MOVING THROUGH

LIFE TRANSITIONS

WITH POWER AND PURPOSE
SECOND EDITION

Cara DiMarco, Ph.D.
Lane Community College

Prentice Hall
Upper Saddle River, New Jersey 07458

Library of Congress Cataloging-in-Publication Data

DiMarco, Cara.
    Moving through life transitions with power and purpose / Cara
DiMarco. — 2nd ed.
        p.   cm.
    Rev. ed. of: Life transitions.
    Includes bibliographical references and index.
    ISBN 0-13-919465-7
        1. Life change events—Psychological aspects.   2. Change.
(Psychology)   3. Adjustment (Psychology)   I. DiMarco, Cara.   Life
transitions.   II. Title.
BF637.L53D55   2000
155.2'4—dc 21   99–12702
                                                                      CIP

Publisher: *Carol Carter*
Acquisitions Editor: *Sande Johnson*
Managing Editor: *Mary Carnis*
Production: *Holcomb Hathaway, Inc.*
Production Liaison: *Glenn Johnston*
Director of Manufacturing and Production: *Bruce Johnson*
Manufacturing Buyer: *Marc Bove*
Cover Art Director: *Jayne Conte*
Editorial Assistant: *Michelle M. Williams*
Marketing Manager: *Jeff McIlroy*
Marketing Assistant: *Barbara Rosenberg*

© 2000, 1995 by Prentice-Hall, Inc.
Upper Saddle River, New Jersey 07458

This book was previously published under the title *Life Transitions:
Finding Your Way Over, Under, Around, and Through Life's Challenges.*

Printed in the United States of America

11 12 13 14 15

ISBN 0-13-919465-7

Prentice-Hall International (UK) Limited, *London*
Prentice-Hall of Australia Pty. Limited, *Sydney*
Prentice-Hall Canada Inc., *Toronto*
Prentice-Hall Hispanoamericana, S.A., *Mexico*
Prentice-Hall of India Private Limited, *New Delhi*
Prentice-Hall of Japan, Inc., *Tokyo*
Pearson Education Asia Pte. Ltd., *Singapore*
Editora Prentice-Hall do Brasil, Ltda., *Rio de Janeiro*
Prentice-Hall, Upper Saddle River, *New Jersey*

Dedication

To all my teachers,
who believed it's not what you know,
it's what you're willing to learn.
To all the Transitions to Success students,
who taught me through their openness and courage
and shared their wisdom and joy.
And to Bob and Spike,
who helped me heal,
helped me know my power,
and cheered me on
from one transition
to another.

CONTENTS

MOVING THROUGH

LIFE TRANSITIONS

WITH POWER AND PURPOSE

SECOND EDITION

WHO IS THIS BOOK DESIGNED FOR?

This book is designed for adults who are facing significant life transitions and want some assistance in moving more smoothly through their current and future life transitions.

More specifically, this book is designed for people who would like help with:

* dealing with the intense emotions and lowered self-esteem that transitions often bring
* building useful coping skills, behaviors, and emotional responses
* developing healthier relationships
* predicting and preparing for future transitions
* discovering their typical reactions to change
* establishing a new sense of direction and purpose while moving through the transition process

My philosophy in writing this book stems from my work as a college professor and psychologist—namely that life is full of wonderful learning opportunities and the more we can understand ourselves and our experiences, the more we can make sense of our painful experiences and actively strive to create more joyful experiences in our lives. Much of what I witness in the work I do with students and clients is the fear and pain that undergoing life transitions creates for them. The fear and pain occur simply because it is frightening and painful to go through changes when we are unable to make sense of the change process itself and its impact on us.

The best way I know to reduce pain, fear, and the resulting confusion, indecisiveness, and inaction is to increase your level of self-knowledge and self-awareness. And this book is written with exactly that goal in mind—that by truly knowing yourself, knowing your emotional reactions, your strengths and limitations, your values, your style in relating to others, and numerous other pieces of self-awareness—that you can reduce the fear and pain in your life by knowing yourself and knowing what helps and hinders you as you move through change.

And as you know yourself more thoroughly, you are then able to live in the world in a more honest and real way, with your energy freed up to live in the present moment, neither regretting the past nor fearing the future. My intention in keeping this book brief in length comes from a twofold awareness: (1) that in times of transition, usually your focus and attention span is shortened due to the stress and demands of the transition, and (2) my belief that you are your own best expert, that you possess the answers for how to have your transitions and life run more smoothly, and this book can serve to bring your self-knowledge into focus. If you need additional information on any topic, please refer to the recommended readings (and instructors will find additional exercises for each chapter included in the instructor's manual), but I encourage you to bring the focus consistently back to yourself. What you need to know is inside of you. Much of life is simply a remembering of truths that you've forgotten or let slip away. Working your way through this book will help you create a life that works for you.

HOW TO GET THE MOST OUT OF THIS BOOK

The goal of this book is to provide a framework for transitions that you can personalize based on your own patterns, tendencies, and characteristics. This personalized framework will allow you to construct a relatively predictable transition process that incorporates the best of your self-knowledge and strengths along with your awareness of your own personal pitfalls and potholes. You can get the most out of this book by reading through each chapter and doing all of the written exercises before moving to the next chapter. I encourage you to resist the tendency to simply read the questions rather than writing out your answers. The secret to smoothly navigating transitions lies in your written responses.

There you will find the keys to making your current and future transitions more manageable.

This book is designed to assist you in moving to a place of clarity and action. Each chapter includes questions and awareness prescriptions to help you apply the information presented and move from feeling as though your transitions are happening to you to feeling that you have the power and the ability to create and achieve what you want in life. Use the empty journal pages provided in the back of this book to record your responses to the questions you encounter as you read.

My job is to provide the framework and systematic exercises that will lead you through self-discovery and self-assessment. Your part in this is to answer all of the questions as fully and honestly as possible. Working together, we can help you make sense out of your life transitions and move through them with power and purpose.

Are you ready? Good. Let's begin this exciting and growth-inducing journey.

DEFINING TRANSITIONS

CHANGES VS. TRANSITIONS

You may face many transitions during the course of your life. These transitions include marriage, divorce, childbirth, an empty nest, addiction recovery, beginning and ending careers, starting school again, a loss of health, the death of a loved one, relocating, and an endless variety of personal failures and successes that can create change in your life.

Despite the differences in each of these transitions, some commonalities exist. All transitions consist of loss—a loss of what was familiar and known, a loss of certainty, a loss of opportunities, and a loss of personal history and what used to be. Sometimes especially painful transitions will bring a loss of a sense of yourself, a loss of perspective, and a loss of hope.

It is crucial to remember that these losses will loom larger and seem more unbearable in the early stages of transition. Often, it is not until the middle or later stages of transition that you begin to experience a sense of excitement and adventure regarding new opportunities for positive growth and change in your life.

Unfortunately, you generally are faced with grieving for all that you are losing before you are able to celebrate all the positive things that you stand to gain. If you can remind yourself of this in the early stages of your transition, you can alleviate much of the hopelessness and maintain a more positive outlook. A simple way to remember this is with the saying, "First pain, then gain." This can help remind you that pain and loss are unavoidable and can also encourage you to work through these feelings so that you can incorporate the gains into your life. Chapter Three can assist you in dealing with the fear and loss inherent in transitions, and Chapter Eight can help you integrate the awareness, knowledge, strength, and growth you've gained in going through your transition.

So how do you know if you're really going through a transition or if what you're experiencing is actually many small changes? Are there differences between changes and transitions?

Although changes and transitions are related to one another, there *are* differences between the two. A transition is a major reshaping of your day-to-day existence, a redefining of your roles, a reconceptualizing of your picture of yourself, and a reworking of how you conduct your life. Most transitions involve some altering of your identity: beginning or ending a relationship, starting a new career, the birth of a child, or returning to school. A change is a shift in what you're used to, a variation in your habits or your approach to situations. Changes are things like having your work schedule shifted, deciding to start an exercise program, or learning to make your own car repairs. And although changes may affect you in the moment, changes don't disrupt your life to the magnitude that transitions often do.

All transitions consist of loss—
a loss of what was familiar and known.

Think about the difference between changing a habit versus altering your whole way of life—starting to eat healthy foods versus becoming a parent. The difference lies in the fact that, at least initially, you can make a number of changes in your eating habits, and people are probably going to perceive you as continuing to be the same person that they have known. However, once you move through a life transition such as becoming a parent, you may alter how you are in the world to such a significant extent that others may not feel they know you as thoroughly in your new roles.

Although there are significant differences between changes and transitions, small changes can lead a person to the edge of transition. Not all changes result in a transition occurring, but all transitions incorporate a series of changes. That is why transitions are so challenging—because they consist of many different changes often made over a short

Figure 1.1

"Wilbur, try a little change—it'll be good for you."

period of time. Most of us can handle one or two small changes at a time, even though we may not enjoy making those changes. Where most of us jam up, feel overwhelmed, and panic is when what we are facing seems like an unending tidal wave of significant changes.

Several things can help with the unjamming process. First, remember that change is about action and transition is about process. While you often can enact change quickly by taking action, transition usually involves a longer unfolding or developing of a new phase of your life that can't be completed or resolved in a day or a week. Anything you can do to remind yourself of that and minimize your impatience to complete the transition will make the process go more smoothly.

Second, be clear about your own values and beliefs about change and transition. Are they primarily positive or negative events? What did you learn from your family about dealing with change and transition? How do you view your ability to cope with transition?

Third, it is possible to build your tolerance for facing transitions by remembering that you can break down each transition into smaller change components that you *can* handle. If that still feels too difficult, you can build your capacity for change by deliberately practicing changing small aspects of your life that create minimal anxiety. Remember, you improve with practice, and if what you've practiced is avoiding change, you now have the chance to practice getting good at dealing with change. An important part of dealing well with change is having a framework for making sense out of what is happening to you. We'll look at that in the next section of this chapter. First, let's take a look at some of your thoughts and feelings about changes and transitions:

Q

1. Complete the following sentences:
   - When I hear the word change, I

     ....

     ....

A

   - The worst thing about change is

     ....

     ....

   - The best thing about change is

     ....

     ....

2. What changes have you made in the past year and how difficult or easy were those changes?

   ....

   ....

3. Are there any small changes that you want to be making now?

   ....

   ....

4. What transitions are you facing or currently experiencing?

   ....

   ....

5. What level of trust do you have in your ability to handle changes and transitions?

   ....

   ....

EXPLORING DIFFERENT TRANSITION MODELS

A number of transition frameworks, or models, have been constructed to help make sense of the transition process. It's important to remember that there is no one right or true transition framework. Each one is merely a model of what comprises the transition process; each makes best sense to the author who generated that particular model. Let's discuss two models that contain some important transition components, as well as a couple of transition metaphors. I will then share my own transition framework. I encourage you to utilize what makes most sense to you and discard the rest. The important point is that you have some kind of an image of what the transition process looks like so you can have some point of reference about where you are in your process.

One transition model, developed by William Bridges, looks at transition as a three-part process. Every transition starts with an ending of something, followed by a neutral zone, then another beginning. What I especially like about Bridges's model is the upfront reminder that every transition unavoidably contains an ending followed eventually by another beginning. That concept is one of the hardest things to remember in the midst of change, yet remembering it can generate a good deal of comfort during times of transition.

The transition process is like being on a trapeze.

Another useful transition model is a seven-stage transition curve proposed by Spencer and Adams. They devised a mood curve to represent the fact that most people experience a significantly low period in the middle of their transitions, followed by later stages in which their moods improve. The low-mood stage is called "the pit," which is an apt description of the swampy emotions most people encounter in the darkest moment of their transitions. I think that it's especially helpful to remember that this stage is a normal, expected aspect of a transition; Spencer and Adams provide a useful perspective on the importance of not trying to bypass this stage.

If images help you visualize concepts and understand them more fully, then the following two metaphors might work well for you. One metaphor is that the transition process is like being on a trapeze. The old way of life is the bar you start out holding onto, the new part of your life that you're entering is the other bar that you're getting ready to grasp, and when you're flying through the air, you experience the void after one aspect of your life has ended and before another has begun.

A second transition metaphor compares the process of going through a transition to the process of a caterpillar becoming a butterfly. The caterpillar starts to move out of its caterpillar way of life, builds a cocoon, and later emerges into a new phase of life as a butterfly. The cocoon portion of this process is when the major transformations take place, when the caterpillar grows into a new role and a new way of being in the world.

My transition framework is based on a documentary film about the cliff divers of Acapulco. I was up late at night watching this film because my boyfriend had just informed me that our relationship was over and that he was moving on. So there I was, curled up in the rocker, staring fixedly at the television, barely focusing on the screen, wondering what I was going to do next. At some point, the narrator's voice cut through my panicked internal chatter to explain how new cliff divers are trained. As I watched the process, I was struck by how terrified the young boys looked, how impossible scaling the rocks leading up to the cliff seemed, and how unthinkable it was to dive headfirst into the water below.

Then, sitting there huddled in the dark, I realized that the boys and I were going through the same feelings and largely the same process; the only difference was that the boys had someone to guide them through the process and I had only myself. That's when I decided to devise my own guide manual to help me through those points in my transition when I was struggling to figure out what to do. What I am going to share next with you is exactly what has helped me make it through some especially tough transitions.

Start by looking at the drawing of the transition framework in Figure 1.2. Notice the road that enters from the right side of the page. That road

Figure 1.2

Transition cliff-diving model.

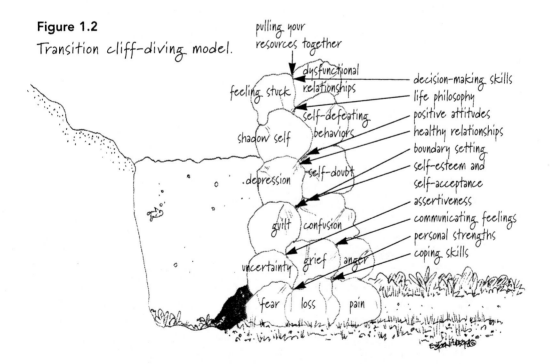

connects back to whatever phase of your life you're leaving and gets you to the base or beginning of your next transition. All sorts of events could have sent you down this road: discontent (yours or someone else's); the feeling that parts of your life aren't working; a forced change of circumstances—death, divorce, job loss, children leaving home; a desire for something more, to grow and improve your life; or any other significant event or want that leads you to the edge of a transition.

You've heard the expression "at the end of my rope." Well, you're now "at the end of your road," standing at the base of an enormous, towering pile of rocks leading to a narrow cliff at the very top. When you're at the base of this monstrous pile of rocks, you're facing something that you've never done before—making a specific life transition. Although you may have gone through a similar transition before, you have never had to make exactly the same changes that this transition requires. One of the toughest moments in the transition process comes when you face the overwhelming mass of rocklike barriers over which you must maneuver to reach the diving point for your next transition. These rock barriers consist of the feelings and behaviors that are the most difficult for you to deal with, often the very feelings and behaviors that prevent your life and relationships from working well.

Before you can even begin to deal with the rocks and boulders of your transition, you need to feel certain that your basic survival needs are met. These survival needs include food, water, clothing, and shelter. Without them, you cannot reasonably expect to have the physical and emotional resources to effectively contend with your current transition. You may need to park yourself at the side of the road near the base of the boulders and give yourself permission to not grapple with the emotional boulders of your transition until you have made certain your basic survival needs have been met. Once that has been accomplished, you can move back to the seemingly overwhelming mass of boulders and begin dealing with them as you move through your transition.

So, what makes these rocks seem so overwhelming? For one thing, because these rock barriers are composed of feelings and behaviors that are difficult to deal with, you may have an enormous amount of practice avoiding them, and very little experience successfully dealing with them. In times of transition, however, it is virtually impossible to avoid grappling your way through feelings that you may otherwise sidestep in calmer moments. To make the most of your transition, it is essential to confront each rock barrier as it emerges before you, and to remember that you just can't leap to the top of the cliff without experiencing, expressing, and processing the feelings and behaviors represented by each of the rocks. Your rock barriers looming before you may look slightly different from the ones I am about to describe. If so, that's fine. You'll have an opportunity to label the rocks to correspond with the barriers you face later in Chapter Two.

Look at Figure 1.2 again. Start at the base of the rock pile and notice the large labeled rocks along with small handholds and footholds that are also labeled. I'll come back to the handholds and footholds after discussing the large rocks. I've labeled the feelings and experiences on the rocks in the order that one individual might experience them. Let's imagine that this person first encounters feelings of fear, loss, and pain when she faces a new transition. Once she deals with these feelings, she moves on to working her way through her uncertainty, grief, and anger. And so she continues, slowly working her way up the cliff, sometimes slipping, sometimes making headway.

Just as the aspiring cliff divers contend with climbing up slippery, wet rocks, so you also face the same slippery task. Just as you feel as though you are making headway, you can slip and find that you've slid back down to rocks that you thought you left behind long ago. There is no straight path or easy way up to the top of the cliff. You need to proceed one step at a time.

Intention and attention will help you move to higher rocks and help you regain your focus when you slip and lose your footing. Intention and attention refers to having the intention to feel what you need to feel to move up the rocks, and having the attention to notice what each rock asks of you and the opportunities offered by each one. Each step of the transition over the rocks is a choice—how you'll approach it, when you'll tackle it, what your attitude will be, how open you are to learning from the experience, and how long you'll focus on each step. The best you can do is try not to blindly rush your way over the rocks; pay attention to rocks that might be especially slippery for you, and remember that you can slip without losing your grip altogether.

* * *

Remember that you can slip without losing your grip altogether.

* * *

Sounds pretty bleak, doesn't it? But you can do much to minimize your concerns about losing your grip. One thing you can do to increase your stability as you climb over the rocks is to pick the handholds and footholds that you're going to rely on as you make your way up to the top of the cliff. These handholds and footholds consist of coping strategies,

Figure 1.3

Only you have the right to judge the quality of your transition.

personal strengths, abilities, and life skills that you can draw on or develop to help you move over and past each rock that stands between you and the top of the cliff. They include communicating feelings, assertiveness, self-esteem, boundary setting, self-acceptance, healthy relationships, positive attitudes, personal life philosophy, decision making, risk taking, the ability to pull your resources together, and many other skills and personal attributes. Some of them already exist and are within your grasp, making your climb a bit more manageable. Other footholds and handholds may need to be created on the spot, carefully chipped out in mid-maneuver, just when you feel least able to tackle a new task or learn a new skill.

Remember that it's not a sheer, straight climb with no time to catch your breath. There will be ledges on which you can rest and take stock of the steps ahead. If you stand back a little bit, you can see the individual steps involved in dealing with each rock, instead of being overwhelmed by what seems like one unscalable lump. You'll then be able to realize that some of the steps are more manageable than you first thought. And just as you can get pebbles lodged in your shoes, you can unintentionally carry pieces of previous rocks with you. It's important to periodically stop, empty out your shoes, and keep your emotional load as light as you possibly can. Remember, no matter how rushed or panicked you feel about this process, it is essential to climb the rocks one at a time and pause when you need to before climbing the next.

When you make it to the top, you're faced with diving into the new transition, but you don't know what's waiting below. It could be balmy, clear water with bright fish, or it could be sharp rocks, shallow water, and hungry sharks. You're scared to look back down at where you just came from, and you're scared to keep going. And it's ironic, isn't it, that the reward for all of this challenging climbing over emotional rock barriers leads to the ultimate scary moment, which is to walk out to the edge of your transition and dive into your new life. Yet the only way to make it to the opposite shore and the new phase of your life is to continue moving ahead. What are you supposed to do? This is where you pull your resources together and use everything you know to improve your chances of encountering warm water and a gentle current. You do this by observing the conditions around you and timing your dive into the transition as the tide is coming in and the wind is blowing in the right direction so you won't hit bottom.

You also set up safety measures to help you survive any potential unseen risks lurking beneath the surface of your transition. Those measures might include friends in boats to fish you out if you need extra help, flotation rings bobbing on the water's surface, or buoys set up around the perimeter of where you're headed so you know where your boundaries are. It means harnessing the best of your faith, hope, humor, and sturdiness as you ready yourself for the dive into your new life.

When it's time to dive, you take the leap with courage and common sense, reminding yourself how important it is to be willing to enter this brand-new phase of your life. And despite what anyone else may say, if you make contact with the water and you surface, you've then successfully completed your transition. Some people will stand on shore with Olympic scorecards, rating your transition, perhaps even suggesting that you should do it all over again. There is no right or wrong way to accomplish your transition, and all you need to do is paddle to the surface and swim to shore.

When you're on the opposite shore, lying on the warm sand, watching the light and the water mix and move together, breathe deeply and enjoy. You're in that glorious place of relative calm and stability between the transition you've just completed and the one that lies ahead. You're able to enjoy all the positive and exciting aspects of your new transition. In the next section we'll discuss what kinds of transitions are common as you move through your life cycle. Then, in future chapters, we deal one at a time with the rocks, the negative feelings, the handholds, and the life skills as we help you move through your life transition.

Before we move on, consider your responses to the following questions:

Q 1. What feelings and behaviors within yourself do you have the most difficulty with during a transition?

A ....

....

....

2. What do you want most from others when you are going through a transition? To leave you alone, to be good listeners, to seek you out, or something else? Are you able to ask for what you want? Do you have people in your life who give you these things?

....

....

....

CYCLES OF CHANGE ACROSS THE LIFE SPAN

No matter how hard you try to avoid transitions or how much you dislike them and try to structure your life so you go through as few as possible, transitions are basically unavoidable. As things change around you, you begin to change, and you reach turning points in your life where you have to crawl up the rock barriers, face your fear, and make some changes. Fortunately, transitions can be positive, growth-inducing experiences as you learn to maneuver your way over the rock barriers. And while the transitions that you face will depend to some degree on your cultural background, spiritual beliefs, and the country you live in, most of us move through some relatively generic life transitions as we motor through the life cycle.

The transitions of aging occur as we grow older: our physical abilities change, and we come to rely on others. Transitions of relationships occur as old friends and coworkers drift apart, relatives die, marriages begin and end, children leave home, grandchildren move in, and neighbors sell their homes and move away. In addition, there are career transitions as our careers develop and grow, bringing promotions, or as careers become obsolete and our jobs end, or as our interests lead us to pursue different careers, or as we approach retirement.

Transitions also occur in the roles we play: daughter, mother, soldier, waitress, lawyer, auto mechanic, grandmother, welder, wife, widow, city council member. And there are transitions in our internal life as well: in the values we hold, in our guiding beliefs and life philosophy, in how we view ourselves and others, and in our preferences and desires.

One way to clarify how far you've proceeded with your life transitions is to complete the transition lifeline exercise at the end of this section. As you continue reading your way through the remainder of this book, you may remember additional transitions that you'll want to add to your transition lifeline.

I also encourage you to write out your responses to the questions for your journal. Many people shy away from keeping a journal because they think that there is only one way to write it or that they don't know what to say. All you need to do is write down what you're noticing, wondering about, thinking, feeling, or doing. Whatever seems most important to what's going on for you right now should go into your journal. Don't feel limited to only writing your reaction to the journal questions—just use those to get you started and then write about whatever emerges for you. In addition, give yourself permission to write short phrases rather than full sentences, to misspell words, and not to worry about punctuation or correct grammar. Just focus on expressing your thoughts and feelings.

Here's your chance to construct your own transition lifeline. Start with the earliest significant transition you can remember and enter the year the transition occurred on the blank transition lifeline form in Figure 1.4. If you had mainly positive feelings about the transition *during* the time of the transition, write the name of the transition above the line. If you had primarily negative feelings about the transition at the time it occurred, write the name of the transition below the line (see the example in Figure 1.5). Continue doing this for each significant transition until you have reached your current transition.

Next, think about how you feel about each transition *now*. Put a plus sign by each transition that you feel positive about now, even though that may not match how you felt about it at the time it was happening. Put a minus sign by the transitions that you feel negative about now. Finally, look at each transition and decide which (if any) transitions you freely and consciously chose. Put a star by those transitions.

Is there any kind of dominant trend or pattern to your transitions that you can see? Don't worry if no clear pattern appears because we will deal more with patterns in Chapter Two. Just make your best guess and try to describe what you notice.

Here are some exercises that will help you begin to personalize the information presented in this chapter. Begin by writing yourself a prescription for self-awareness.

Figure 1.4

Blank lifeline.

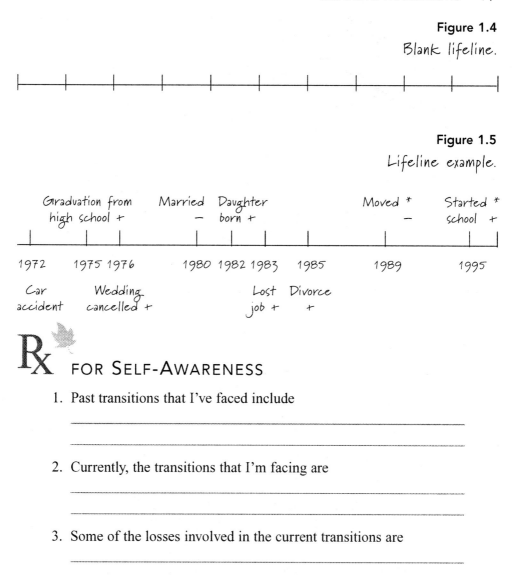

Figure 1.5

Lifeline example.

FOR SELF-AWARENESS

1. Past transitions that I've faced include

   _____

   _____

2. Currently, the transitions that I'm facing are

   _____

   _____

3. Some of the losses involved in the current transitions are

   _____

   _____

4. Things I could gain from these transitions are

   _____

   _____

5. The outcomes I most want from these transitions are

   _____

   _____

6. The biggest fears I have about these transitions are

....

....

7. Resources and strengths that I currently possess are

....

....

8. New resources I'd like to create to help me are

....

....

9. Beliefs that help sustain me through hard times include

....

....

10. In the past, I've viewed transitions as

....

11. In the future, I'd like to see transitions as

....

FOR YOUR JOURNAL . . .

1. What did you learn about yourself from this chapter?
2. How does that change things for you or help you make sense of your life?
3. What else do you want to know about yourself?

RECOMMENDED READINGS

Bridges, William. 1980. *Transitions.* New York: Addison-Wesley.

Focuses on the three major stages of transition and describes aspects of endings, the in-between neutral zone, and beginnings.

Spencer, Sabina and Adams, John. *Life Changes.* San Luis Obispo, CA: Impact Publishers.

Describes a seven-stage mood curve for transition and includes some brief questions to assist the reader with self-exploration.

MAKING SENSE OUT
OF CHANGE

Smooth stumbles
Fluid errors
change flows into itself
and on
and I learn to ride the waves
hold my course
but not too tightly
give up a sense of balance
for a chance to grow.

From "Unattached" 1981

RANGE OF REACTIONS TO CHANGE

How do you respond to change? Do your reactions to change hinder your progress through your life transitions? Are you aware of any pattern in your reactions to change? Do you remember how Chapter One described the difference between change and transition? From this point forward, for the sake of simplicity, the word *change* will be used to refer to the change process that occurs *within* major life transitions.

One of the most pertinent issues concerning change in the transition process is how individuals respond to change. As a psychologist and college instructor, I am continually amazed by the range of reactions that people display in response to the experience of change in their lives. Some individuals gravitate toward change, feel stagnant without it, and become bored, dreary, and restless when there is too much continuity and consistency in their lives. Other individuals despise change and will endure intolerable situations to escape contending with the anxiety, panic, and dread that change conjures up in them.

There are no right or wrong reactions to change. What is crucial to examine, however, is whether your particular reactions to change enhance or diminish your quality of life. Certain responses to change are more functional in terms of assisting you in moving toward goals you have established for yourself. Less useful reactions undermine your progress or cause you to lose highly valued opportunities and relationships. As you read through this chapter, consider whether your reaction to change diminishes your life in any respect, and what aspects of your existence are damaged. It can be invaluable to rethink how you respond to change. Pull out a piece of paper and a pencil and write down any awareness you gain as you read through the following list of common reactions to change.

Duck and Cover

Essentially, the core belief embedded in this reaction is, "If I hunker down and pull the blanket over my head, maybe when I emerge, everything will be back to normal." The notion is that if you withdraw from everything, if you take yourself out of the flow of change, perhaps the change will stop. Often this reaction stems from the desire to rewind the videotape of your life back to the place before the change began. This line of reasoning implies that if you climb out of the river and sit on the bank, maybe the river will stop flowing. Unfortunately, neither the river nor the change process works that way. Change continues whether or not we hide from it.

If your response to change is to step back and gain some perspective, that may help you analyze your situation objectively. However, if you tend to take a foxhole approach to change, you can sabotage yourself by failing to capitalize on opportunities; you may want to reexamine your options for responding to change.

If you need to retreat during times of change, how can you indulge that without allowing it to interfere with what you need to accomplish? The trick is to structure activities that let you disappear for only a limited time. Some possible options include hiding out in the dark at the

Figure 2.1

Change occurs no matter how well you try to hide from it.

movies, taking a warm bath in a softly lit bathroom, sitting in the dark with candles flickering—anything that allows you to remain quiet and step out of the change for a few moments.

If you take a foxhole approach to change, you can sabotage yourself by failing to capitalize on opportunities.

The Best Defense Is a Hostile Offense

This reaction to change occurs when an individual feels emotionally unequipped to deal with the anxiety and fear that accompany most change. Rather than acknowledge and feel that fear, the individual will deny any fearful feelings and instead will express anger. This person deals with anxiety and upheaval by being irritable, mean-tempered, fault-finding, and cynical. Basically, the core belief of this reaction is, "Everything is changing, it's someone else's fault, and someone is going to pay for it." This individual finds acknowledging the change and experiencing the related sadness, grief, and fear to be so painful and threatening that lashing out in anger is the only way to achieve self-protection.

To a degree, a portion of that response is quite reasonable. Being angry, frustrated, and blaming is understandable because it is painful to have to readjust how you function in the world. Whether it's carving out a new niche, finding different ways of relating to the people around you, or learning new skills, if you didn't choose the transition, your impulse to be blaming and angry may be especially strong.

One significant drawback to this style of responding to change is that it makes it difficult to maintain close relationships. Even if people truly love you and want to assist you through your change, after awhile, even the most supportive person will grow weary of the hostility and choose to leave the relationship. If this is your reaction to change, it's important to consider safe avenues for expressing your fear and anxiety and dealing with it directly. You might consider expressing your feelings through writing, dancing, painting, music, exercise, singing, or any other creative outlet.

Change? I'm Not Going Through Any Change!

The individual who adopts this stance responds to major life changes by refusing to recognize that anything has changed; therefore this person does not alter any significant aspect of day-to-day living. Instead, it's business as usual, with no acknowledgment that any disruption has occurred or that action might be needed to deal with the ramifications of the change. When you ask this individual if everything's okay, the answer invariably is, "Well, of course, why wouldn't everything be okay?"

This denial-based reaction to change can be very adaptive in a work environment, where it is important to proceed with work projects despite major upheavals in your personal life. However, it can generate problems of chaotic proportions in change situations requiring immediate decision or action. An individual with this reaction to change could receive an eviction notice and respond to the impending change by continuing to get up each morning, go through the motions at work, and return home in the evening without searching for a new residence. Although a small amount of denial might allow an individual to continue to meet important responsibilities, an excess of denial will lead to more disruptions in the long run. The secret lies in giving yourself permission to deny change when doing so won't interfere with fulfilling career and personal obligations, while also forcing yourself to snap out of denial and confront reality when this is essential to your survival.

Help Me, I'm Helpless, I Can't Help It

Another reaction to change occurs when an individual confronted with change freezes, panics, and then collapses. Faced with the anxiety of coping with significant change, this person folds up like a house of cards, caves in, and is immobilized. Someone who engages in this reaction style may not openly indicate her panic, and others may not realize that anything is wrong until she fails to appear at work, pay her bills, or pick up the kids from school. The intention behind this style is healthy—to make others aware of your difficulties in dealing with change and your need for support and assistance. The dysfunctional aspect of this style is the belief that you can obtain assistance only when you are incapacitated.

Some family systems teach that the only way to receive any support is by emotionally crumbling. Individuals growing up in this kind of family environment learn that if they show any strength or stability in the midst of change, they will be left to handle everything by themselves. If this was true of your family system, consider the possibility that there are more direct ways of indicating that you need support and assistance that also allow you to demonstrate some of your core strength and resilience. Many people out in the world are happy to help you even when you are capable and coping well with your changes. You don't have to fall apart to get people's attention. In fact, people are generally more attracted to someone who demonstrates strength than they are to someone who constantly portrays helplessness and an incapacity to cope with stress.

Drama + Chaos = Excitement

The person engaged in this reaction chooses to depict every change as a dramatic catastrophe filled with intrigue and danger. Every situation is painted in large, vivid strokes—a broken arm becomes a brush with paralysis. One of the positive aspects of this style is that it exposes acquaintances and coworkers to some highly entertaining, dramatic accounts of dangerously close calls. However, if you are intimately connected to the person, this style can become exhausting because it affords no sense of any gradation of change: everything occurs in huge proportions and at a frantic pace. The person who uses this style finds that people eventually stop reacting to the significance of the change because they feel manipulated by the continual drama and chaos. Another drawback is that using this style drowns out the ability to notice small, quiet opportunities and information that could help the transition proceed more smoothly because nothing gets attended to but the big, chaotic details.

If this is your style, it is important that you acknowledge that you often create drama out of merely an unfortunate situation. For instance, if you receive an eviction notice, this dramatic style might lead you to tell your landlord to get lost and then remain in the apartment until the police arrive, break down your door, and arrest you. Although this behavior will certainly allow you to relate some dramatic stories, it might be more advantageous to focus on containing and minimizing aspects of the change rather than cultivating them.

I'm Too Depressed to Blink, Much Less Care

The central belief behind this reaction to change is that if you stop feeling, wanting, and being actively alive—if you numb your emotions, movements, and awareness—perhaps you can freeze things in place and stop the process of change. This is a natural reaction not only for humans but for many other animals as well. Think about what animals do when they feel threatened: they freeze, remain motionless, attempt to blend into the environment, and seemingly hope that they don't have to contend with the threatening predator.

Despite the useful application of this behavior, one significant drawback is that once you are fully immobilized, it is very difficult to remobilize yourself to grapple with the changes effectively. You can assist yourself by exploring what thoughts and behaviors help you reenergize yourself. Most individuals eventually jump-start themselves out of immobility; however, you can accelerate that process by developing your personal list of what helps get you going again.

Achieve, Achieve, a.k.a. I'll Just Work Harder

The individual who reacts in this style acknowledges that change is occurring and responds by saying, "Fine, I'm just going to stay busy and accomplish as much as I can by working harder, faster, and more efficiently until the change blows over." The underlying attitude is, "Of course there is a lot going on, but I'm handling everything splendidly and relatively effortlessly."

On one level, this is spectacularly functional because individuals who use this style get an incredible number of tasks and projects accomplished, and they are highly valued by employers and coworkers. Unfortunately, in the process of achieving so much, they avoid facing and dealing with their emotions. This avoidance often leads to physical illness—ulcers, chronic headaches, racing heart, digestive difficulties—

because the emotional stress triggered by the changes eventually cannot be repressed and leaks out through illness that cannot be ignored. If this is your style, retain what you do well, but locate someone or some environment where it's safe to be less than superhuman and allow yourself to express your emotions. You might consider reframing this as a form of achievement—that feeling your emotions fully is a major achievement and it is absolutely compatible with being competent.

I'm Doomed No Matter What I Do

This fatalistic reaction to change operates from the perspective that no matter what a person does, life will continue to be a series of neutral to bad experiences, with changes comprising a substantial number of those bad experiences. This person feels that some of the change that occurs will result in tolerable outcomes and other change will not, and nothing can be done to affect the outcome. Although a portion of this stance is accurate in the sense that change *is* going to happen no matter what we do, the belief that there is nothing we can do to affect the outcome of the change is inaccurate.

You must assess what you can and cannot do.

In addition to being inaccurate, this belief blinds people to the endless options, actions, and decisions that could alter circumstances into more appealing outcomes. Although it is healthy to be aware of the limits of your personal power, it is unhealthy to fail to recognize and use the power you do possess. You must assess what you can and cannot do, alter what you can, obtain assistance when appropriate, and attempt to accept and deal with the things you are unable to influence. And remember, no matter how unalterable the change is, we always have the power to choose and shape our attitude toward change.

I May Not Like It, But I Can Handle It

The final reaction to change is the most useful and adaptive approach to dealing with change. This reaction is based on the notion that things are going to be continually changing—sometimes in small, imperceptible ways, and sometimes in larger, global, all-encompassing ways—and that you are capable of dealing effectively with the circumstances that change brings. In addition, since change occurs within you as well as around you, you realize and accept that there is no sense in attempting to avoid change because it is impossible to fully avoid change in yourself.

* *

There is always something positive to be learned from change.

* *

Instead you continue to remind yourself that you are an integral part of the change process, and that you can notice and deal with change in a variety of effective ways. Some change will work out wonderfully, and some change won't. Yet there is always something positive to be learned from change. Finally, don't forget to seek support when needed, and don't neglect celebration when you've successfully faced the challenge of change.

WHAT'S NORMAL?

What's normal in terms of your reactions to change? It is absolutely normal to dread change, to attempt to minimize it, and to feel an immense amount of anxiety. It is also normal to do anything that partially or totally stops the change process—to search for ways to escape it physically, emotionally, mentally. Doing nearly anything is normal, with the exception of engaging in things that are harmful to yourself or others.

On the other hand, there is a significant difference between what is normal and what is healthy. It is normal to behave in ways that clearly aren't in your best interest. Realize, however, that you are reacting to change, and there is nothing wrong with you as a person, even if you could respond to change in ways that would be much more functional than your current responses.

In addition, it is normal to:

* feel that you want to get through the change as quickly as possible
* feel victimized by change and think, "Why is this happening to me? I didn't do anything to deserve this."

* want to find someone to blame for causing the change
* have lingering wishes, feelings, and yearnings for the "good old days"; recall your past experience in a more positive light and idealize what was, in reality, only mediocre
* feel dread about the ramifications of the change and what lies ahead
* feel alternating lethargy and bursts of energy, or terror and excitement
* look at the future with a mixture of optimism, pessimism, and cynicism
* view change as the worst and the best thing that ever happened to you
* feel both that life is over and that it has just begun

It is healthy to examine what your normal or typical reaction to change is and explore whether you can uncover your personal patterns in the process. Once you are able to identify your personal reaction patterns to change, you are equipped to examine whether your reactions are useful or damaging. You can then retain the useful responses and build on those strengths.

You also have the opportunity to consider what aspects of your reactions need rethinking, and you can experiment with responses that could make your transitions more manageable. In other words, by clearly identifying your personal patterns, you can keep what works well and discard the remainder. I know that it is not very appealing to think about adding more changes in the midst of a transition; however, I guarantee that if you start looking at personal patterns, your transitions will be much smoother over the long run. Ready to give it a try?

IDENTIFYING PERSONAL PATTERNS

Many people feel frightened to examine their emotional inner workings and are reluctant to focus closely on their habitual responses to various life events. One of the most common fears is that if you look too closely at your personal patterns, you could discover that you are as awful as you fear or as someone has said you are. Another fear is that other people might also start looking more closely at you and realize how flawed you are. I've yet to meet anyone who didn't express some fear about increasing her awareness of who she truly is without any facades or masks. And another major fear many people have is that all this self-examination will bring an immense amount of pain with no relief and no growth on the other side. But this simply isn't true.

First, pain isn't bottomless or unending, although in the moment it often feels that way. You can handle the feelings that arise from your self-exploration and should your feelings seem too overwhelming to handle on your own, you can seek out the support of caring friends, family, and professionals trained to assist with transitions.

Second, usually what people discover is that they are sturdier and healthier than they thought they were. Looking at personal patterns lets you view your strengths. Most people get themselves into trouble when they overuse their strengths, and it is normal in times of stress to do exactly that. When people feel scared or anxious, they tend to do more of whatever behavior they excel at. If they are outstanding communicators, they will overload others with their nonstop communication. If they are responsible, they will become hyperresponsible and overmanage everything. If they are exceptionally clean and organized, they will overorganize everyone and everything.

It is also important to clarify how you view change. We will conduct a full-fledged exploration of values in Chapter Seven, but before we proceed with the intervening chapters, it is important to gain a clear perspective on your values and beliefs regarding change.

Figure 2.2

Pat was impressed with Robin's zest for cleaning until she was sucked up by Robin's vacuum.
Overusing your strengths can turn them into liabilities.

Q   1. How was change looked at in your family? Was change something that pulled people together? Did they talk about their feelings and face it as a challenge that everyone was going to overcome? Or did people in your family tend to panic, often collapsing and losing their coping skills?

A   _____
    _____
    _____

2. Take a moment to think about some major change that occurred in your childhood. Write that change down.

    _____
    _____
    _____

3. Now think about how the family handled the change. What were some of the prevailing emotions and beliefs shared, and what was the atmosphere around the house? Was it positive and action-oriented? Was it negative and scary? Jot down as many descriptive words as you can think of that summarize that experience. What did that experience of change teach you about how people handle change?

    _____
    _____
    _____

4. Now turn your focus to how you currently view change. Can you discern any carryover effect into your current beliefs regarding change? Is change usually a positive or negative experience for you? Is change something to anticipate or dread?

    _____
    _____
    _____

Draw a line down the center of a sheet of paper and on one side make a list of the things in your life you would be unwilling to change. On the other side, list the things in your life that you would be willing to change. Look at those two lists and notice that they provide an indicator of what you value and what is less important to you.

An additional component in uncovering personal patterns is identifying what kinds of painful experiences keep occurring in your life. In other words, what episodes of pain do you keep replaying? This might mean examining how you manage to continually become involved with partners who, for whatever reason, are unable to remain employed and contribute their financial share to the relationship. It also means exploring your role in developing and maintaining this personal pattern.

Another painful pattern could be that you tend to withdraw in the face of change and emotionally distance yourself from friends. Something that you might want to explore is whether every time you go through a major life change and then reemerge, you have friends who are angry at you and want to end the relationship. You might want to consider why you feel compelled to construct an entire new batch of friends every time you go through a life change. In some situations this is an excellent response, such as if your transition was a decision to recover from substance abuse and you need to establish a new set of friends who aren't using substances.

If you continue to lose friends that you'd rather keep, then it is time to ask yourself about your personal pattern that appears over and over again in the face of change. What strengths do you overdo? What beliefs do you have regarding change? How do those help you? Hinder you? What is the worst thing about change?

Remember, there is no single correct answer to these questions. For one person, the worst aspect of change is not knowing the new rules on how to be or behave. For another person, feeling alone will be the worst part of change. Just keep digging until you uncover your personal patterns.

Two of the most significant benefits of identifying your personal patterns are that they assist you in (1) knowing your own predictable stages of what you go through in the midst of change and (2) determining what behaviors, beliefs, and actions you need to incorporate to make your changes smoother.

Let's start to make your growing self-awareness more cohesive and concrete. Remember the cliff-diving metaphor for change in Chapter One? Figure 2.3 is a blank copy of the cliff rocks. With the blank cliff rocks in front of you, think about some of the rocks or barriers that emerge from your personal patterns. These can include any feelings or behaviors that interfere with you handling change and having your life function smoothly. Write those personal barriers on the rocks. Those barriers might be things like shutting out support or fear of closeness.

Figure 2.3

Blank cliff rocks.

Use a pencil and write each barrier on a separate rock. Don't worry about the order; simply focus on labeling each rock with some aspect of your response to change that hinders your ability to deal effectively with change. Your next step is to think about the handholds, the abilities and skills you would like to be able to utilize as you make your way over each rock. These handholds can include abilities you currently possess as well as those you wish to develop. Draw a line from each handhold crevice and label each one. Again, don't worry about the order for now.

Here are some exercises that will help you begin to personalize the information presented in this chapter. Begin by writing yourself a prescription for self-awareness.

R̶x̶ FOR SELF-AWARENESS

1. The changes I find easiest to handle are

_____

_____

2. The changes I find hardest to handle are

   ....

   ....

3. When I see change coming I

   ....

   ....

4. When change catches me by surprise

   ....

   ....

5. The change I'm most proud of is

   ....

   ....

6. The change I wish I could do over is

   ....

   ....

7. Strengths I overuse in times of stressful change include

   ....

   ....

8. Abilities I underuse in times of stressful change include

   ....

   ....

9. What I like about how I handle change is

   ....

   ....

10. What I don't like about how I handle change is

    ....

    ....

11. Ways others could help me through this current transition are

    ....

    ....

Feel free to renew your prescriptions periodically or rewrite them to accommodate your current needs and goals.

FOR YOUR JOURNAL . . .

1. What did you learn about yourself from this chapter?
2. How does that change things for you or help you make sense of your life?
3. What else do you want to know about yourself?

RECOMMENDED READINGS

Cloud, Henry. 1993. *Changes that Heal.* Grand Rapids, MI: Zondervan Publishing.

> Explains why people develop emotional and relational problems and discusses how to solve them.

Sher, Barbara. 1986. *Wishcraft.* New York: Ballantine.

> Helps in uncovering skills and abilities, in developing a support network for achieving goals and dreams, and in formulating techniques for continued motivation.

Sills, Judith. 1994. *Excess Baggage.* New York: Viking Press.

> Explores common obstacles people create that prevent them from living satisfying lives, and suggests ways to reduce those obstacles.

Wall, Kathleen and Ferguson, Gary. 1998 *Rites of Passage: Celebrating Life's Challenges.* Hillsboro, OR: Beyond Words Publishing.

> Encourages the reader to view life change as a time of great opportunity that can be navigated with grace and understanding and shares how to harness the energy of transitions.

FACING YOUR
OWN TRANSITIONS

GRIEF AND LOSS

Grief and loss are emotions that our society shies away from acknowledging and expressing. We have definite ideas about how long it is appropriate to grieve the loss of a person in our lives. Other than a few ceremonies connected to death, we don't have many traditions to allow the expression of grief and loss. When some of my close friends have lost beloved pets, the reaction of those around them has been, "It's just an animal—get on with it."

Grief and loss generate feelings of immense powerlessness. The events that cause grief and loss are often things that happen to us rather than things that we've chosen. However, it is also possible to feel grief and loss over your own decisions.

The hardest thing about loss is that any current loss triggers emotional and often physical memories of past losses. Losing what you care greatly about can cause you to let go of people, places, and perceptions, often before you are ready to let go. Loss is about longing and aching, about deeply wanting, and about wishing and waiting for what is no longer accessible and what you can no longer have. Loss is about living with lack—lack of something deeply valued and cherished. Loss can make you wonder if you'll ever be the same again—if you'll ever again feel fully alive, take risks, feel joy, move freely through the world, trust others or yourself, take a chance, or reach out and risk losing again.

Figure 3.1

We learn at an early age that loss is unavoidable. "You have to let go of a cookie if you want the milk."

But as carefully as you may try to live your life and make your choices, loss is unavoidable. You lose every time you make a decision and every time you fail to decide. Every action or inaction automatically excludes some possibilities and enhances other possibilities. Each day you encounter dozens of small losses, and each day you take much of that loss in stride.

Every action or inaction automatically excludes some possibilities and enhances other possibilities.

So why is the loss that accompanies major life transitions so painful, so difficult, so hard to make sense of, so difficult to navigate, and so impossible to move out of? Much of the explanation lies in the fact that the process of transition causes you to take stock of what has been and what will never be again. Loss in the midst of transition often means loss of a significant part of yourself, loss of your way of being in the world, loss of self-awareness, self-knowledge, and loss of the comfort that was part of the familiar terrain of your life. When that terrain changes, waves of loss occur. Concrete losses stem from the transition itself: losses of relationships, jobs, health, and personal and financial resources. In addition there are less tangible losses: loss of certainty, loss of confidence, loss of purpose, and loss of direction. With that loss of direction and the floundering that accompanies it come the first waves of grief.

The intensity of your grief depends on the nature and impact of your current losses and on whether you allowed yourself to grieve past losses. Every current loss can awaken the memories and pain of past losses, regardless of how well or how thoroughly you previously dealt with them. The difference lies in whether you tried to ignore or numb the pain of the initial loss or instead tried to work your way through your grief and truly heal the loss. Experiencing and working through your grief helps you to clarify what is truly important to you and can assist you in creating those things in your life.

It is crucial to let yourself feel your sadness, express it, and let it out.

Grief can be especially painful if as a child you weren't allowed to grieve losses as they occurred and instead buried and stockpiled them. If this is true of you, you may often feel more grief than is appropriate for the current circumstances. This is a good clue that part of what you are experiencing is a mingling of past and current grief.

One thing you can do to feel less overwhelmed is to list all the things you are grieving. Pick one thing and take a small step in expressing the emotions, such as talking with a friend, writing in a journal, or listening to music. Feel free to choose anything that helps you express your feelings.

It is crucial to let yourself feel your sadness, express it, and let it out. This honors and cherishes what has existed, what you had hoped for, and what mattered to you. Others are often uncomfortable with our grief and encourage us to mute it, to not express it around them, to shut if off and be over it. You need to find safe, supportive places and people in your life where you can express your grief. Try asking friends to simply listen to you without trying to cheer you up, or track down a therapist to help you process your grief. You might want to invent a personal tradition or ceremony for acknowledging and expressing your grief. A friend of mine writes down individual words or phrases that describe what she is losing. She then burns the paper with the words on it and sprinkles the ashes in her flower garden as a symbol of how the pain from her past can transform itself into growth and beauty in the future.

You can incur all kinds of losses when you go through transitions. There are the obvious losses of whatever is changing in that moment in your life. You often lose a great deal when you change your life:

- your old view of yourself
- approval and support (emotional and financial)
- connections with experiences and places that were special
- important relationships
- your comfort zone—with both yourself and others
- opportunities (although you gain new ones with your changes)
- your dependence on others

To soften the impact of these losses, try making a memory book that contains all of your memories, thoughts, and feelings about whatever aspect of your life is changing. You can write, draw, glue mementos, or include your memories in whatever form you wish. The purpose of creating a memory book is to provide a way to concretely hold onto a piece of what you ultimately must let go of.

Another thing you can do is keep all the familiar parts of your life that you can without inhibiting the progress of your transition. You can soften the impact of the losses that are occurring by not changing any aspect of your life that is not an immediate, necessary part of your transition.

And remember, the flip side of grief and sorrow is joy. The more fully you are willing to experience your loss and pain, the more room you create for your joy in your life. If you attempt to mute or block your grief, you also mute other emotional responses. By opening yourself fully to experiencing, expressing, and processing grief, you also open yourself to the possibility of experiencing tremendous joy.

LETTING GO OF ROLES, ILLUSIONS, AND OLD DREAMS

Many transitional losses, especially many of the most painful losses, are those of roles, dreams, and illusions. It is difficult to let go of old roles because they are how you define yourself and are often the source of much of your self-worth. When children leave home, for example, parents give up the day-to-day role of parent. While they continue to be parents, the role is different now that the children are no longer in the home.

You also give up the illusions of how you hoped things would be, of how you hoped a relationship, job, or experience would turn out. You might lose old dreams, such as the dream of doing something creative with your life or the dream of an ideal relationship or a loving family. This means letting go of what was or what you hoped would occur and facing what actually *is*.

And with that comes the need to let go of the painful experiences that you survived but never acknowledged, the experiences that you started grieving and never finished, and the experiences that you didn't have the safety and luxury of grieving.

FEAR: DEALING WITH AMBIGUITY AND THE UNKNOWN

One thing that makes change hard for most people and makes facing transitions especially difficult is how afraid people are of feeling fear. People are often so afraid of feeling fear that they paralyze themselves in their transitions. Fear is just a feeling like any other emotion, yet it engenders feelings of powerlessness in many individuals.

Part of what creates that feeling of powerlessness is that many people have recurring feelings in the midst of fear. Often those feelings represent deep childhood fears that had to do with physical or emotional survival. Those individual fears can take the form of feelings:

- No one loves me at all.
- I'm never good enough.
- I'll always be alone.
- If I'm myself, people will always leave.
- I will never get my needs met.

One way to identify a childhood fear is to notice the use of overgeneralizations or absolute words: always, never, totally, at all, forever. These kinds of fears represent some of the sharks and alligators that you can face in the water below as you stand at the top of the transition cliff, readying yourself for the dive into the next phase of your life.

You can minimize the impact of these old fears by arguing with your overgeneralizations. Are you completely certain you will *always* be alone? Can you prove it? Try tackling the worst-case scenario by assuming that you are right—no one loves you. You can survive that feeling even if you hate enduring it. You can also take small steps to start creating the love you want in your life.

Q What small steps could you take right now to reduce the fear that you feel?

_____

_____

_____

A Fear is about not knowing if you are safe, about feeling in danger, and about worrying that you might not come out of the situation intact—physically, mentally, emotionally, or spiritually. The most profound aspect of fear is that it never absolutely disappears; people never evolve to a place where they feel entirely free of fear.

Some fear is good; it's part of what keeps us safe. If I am in a dark parking lot late at night and someone is following me, it's good that I feel fear in that moment. Fear helps you protect yourself against danger and harm.

However, that response is different from fear that comes from not knowing what will happen next. If I have many self-doubts, worries, and feelings of panic about not knowing all of the answers to a current problem, then I may work myself into a state of fear. Fear and excitement create the same physiological arousal state in our bodies. Therefore, how you think about and interpret your pounding pulse, rapid breathing, and adrenaline rush determine whether you label the experience exciting or frightening.

* *

It is normal to feel anxious and a bit fearful
in new situations.

* *

Picture meeting an individual whom you consider attractive and potential dating material. You begin a conversation and notice the physical responses just listed. You can perceive those symptoms as indications of your level of excitement at meeting and interacting with the person. Or you can interpret the same symptoms as a gauge of how anxious and ill at ease you are. One handy technique to experiment with is to reframe your interpretations of anxiousness or fearfulness in social settings by saying to yourself, "I am excited and enjoying this."

Another thing you can do in the face of fear is remind yourself that it is normal to feel anxious and a bit fearful in new situations because you haven't done that particular thing before and you are not certain if things are going to work out. You might tell yourself, "Okay, I'm feeling anxious and I want things to work out well, and I don't like not knowing what will happen next." That is different from giving in to the fear and saying, "I can't cope because this is scary and unfamiliar." Remember, you are never powerless—regardless of the circumstances, you always have the power to change your attitude. Many survivors of the Holocaust attribute their psychological survival to their maintaining the belief that despite being stripped of all outward forms of freedom, they still retained their freedom of thought, feeling, and attitudinal outlook on the inhumane circumstances they faced. This belief allowed them to retain their internal power even in the midst of dehumanizing treatment and the rampant destruction of human life.

Challenge also arises in the generalized ambiguity that occurs in the midst of transitions. This ambiguity is the sense that the future represents a string of unknowns: I don't know if I'm going to live to be 58 or 85; if leaving my relationship will make my life better or worse; if the training that I am pursuing will lead to a fulfilling career. I may have my hopes and beliefs, but I don't know for certain how the details of my life will work out. The good news is that if things don't work out the way you wished, or if you made a choice that you no longer like, you can make a different decision and choose again.

In the midst of transitions, there will be far more unknowns than knowns. Part of facing a transition is facing the fact that you don't get to know everything and accepting the emotions that will accompany this awareness. In addition, it means trusting that you will know what to do in a given situation when it occurs. Even though the future is a series of unknowns, those unknowns will slowly become knowns. Information will emerge and confusion will begin to diminish. And as the situation progresses, either you'll possess the inner knowledge and ability to respond to the situation, or, at the very least, you'll be able to brainstorm resources and options with others.

Our society makes it difficult to not know something. Knowledge is considered essential in our information age. However, it is truly acceptable to simply not know, to be confused, to lack clarity, to have no clue about what turn your life is going to take. Even so, you should have an internal sense of direction, of how you would like things to turn out; and you should do what you can to bring those things about. You can help yourself generate this sense of direction by asking yourself, "If I wasn't confused and knew what I needed to know, what is my best guess of how I would want things to turn out?" Assuming this guess is reasonably accurate, what small steps could you take toward your goal? Which step would you be willing to start today?

Although you would be more comfortable knowing how things will turn out, you rarely get that. It's like paddling a boat across a foggy lake. You set your compass, take your bearings, and start paddling. At any given moment, you may not know where you are; you may even be padding in circles. Yet at some point you will make it across the lake. Even if you end up in a cove you didn't intend, you'll be able to either change your direction to head where you intended or explore what the cove has to offer.

The most important thing about fear and the unknown is that you can deal with it; you have or can develop the skills that will allow you to cope. You may not like or relish how you feel, but you can survive those feelings. You can stay out of helplessness and find all kinds of power: to maintain; to ride the waves; to tread water until clarity comes; to calm and soothe yourself; to give supportive feedback to yourself; and to place supportive people around you.

In order to reduce the pain of loss and endings, you may throw yourself into new beginnings to avoid dealing with the loss. Unfortunately, if you do this, the old losses will come back to haunt you. Often, when you make rash, haphazard choices, the chaos resulting from those choices will distract you, and those choices will usually turn out to be negative, life-diminishing decisions. What can you do if you notice yourself mov-

Figure 3.2

It's okay to not know or see everything.

ing in that direction? Be willing to feel your emotions, get personal or professional support, and remember that you can acknowledge and survive your pain.

Pick a current situation that contains a medium amount of fear and unknowns for you. List all of the things you *do* know despite the unknowns. This can include things like knowing that the current situation will not go on forever; knowing that you don't want to move into a certain living environment; and knowing that you can use certain people as resources and support. Now list anything you can think of that would help to comfort and soothe you as you gain clarity regarding your situation. Your comfort list can include whatever works for you, so don't be concerned with whether others would agree with or judge your list. Include anything that helps you feel better provided it isn't destructive to yourself or others. Now pick three soothing things you can do for yourself this week—and do them.

Here are some exercises that will help you begin to personalize the information presented in this chapter. Begin by writing yourself a prescription for self-awareness.

Rx FOR SELF-AWARENESS

1. When I hear the words loss and grief I

----

2. Past losses I've experienced are

----

3. Losses I face in this transition are

----

4. My childhood experiences with loss and grief taught me

_____

_____

_____

5. How I deal with the unknown is

_____

_____

_____

6. My fears regarding the unknown include

_____

_____

_____

7. Some of the things I still know in the midst of change are

_____

_____

_____

8. Some of the things I still have power over are

_____

_____

_____

9. Safe ways that I can express my grief are

_____

_____

_____

10. A personal tradition or ritual for acknowledging my grief could be

_____

_____

_____

11. Gains awaiting me on the other side of this loss could consist of

_____

_____

_____

FOR YOUR JOURNAL . . .

1. What did you learn about yourself from this chapter?
2. How does that change things for you or help you make sense of your life?
3. What else do you want to know about yourself?

RECOMMENDED READINGS

Jeffers, Susan. 1992. *Feel the Fear and Do It Anyway.* New York: Ballantine.

> Presents techniques for managing fear and indecision while taking appropriate risks, for reducing negative self-talk, and for learning new ways to accomplish goals.

Hickman, Martha Whitmore. 1994. *Healing After Loss: Daily Meditations for Working through Grief.* New York: Avon Books.

> Provides daily affirmation and meditations to ease the grieving process and pave the way for healing to begin.

Kingma, Daphne Rose. 1989. *Coming Apart.* New York: Fawcett Crest.

> Examines the process of endings in important relationships and suggests ways to ease the guilt and emotional pain of leaving a relationship.

Samuels, Arthur, 1998. *Creative Grieving.* Stress Free Publishing.

> Focuses on grief as a passage from one phase of life to another and helps uncover how to nurture oneself through the pain of loss.

Viorst, Judith. 1996. *Necessary Losses.* New York: Simon and Schuster.

> Assists in comprehending and coping with the necessary losses of life as people age and grow.

DEALING
WITH EMOTIONS

ANGER, GUILT, SELF-DOUBT, ANXIETY, DEPRESSION

I doubt you could find anyone on the face of the planet who would say, "I really wish I had more anger, guilt, self-doubt, anxiety, and depression—I feel empty and as though I'm missing something without these wonderful feelings." One thing that is important to consider in any discussion of feelings, whether we consider them positive (happiness, enthusiasm, joy, delight) or negative (depression, anger, fear, grief, guilt), is that all feelings have a purpose.

Ask yourself about the purposes of your feelings. What do they allow you to avoid facing, coping with, or having to deal with? For example, if I have a feeling of shyness in social situations, that feeling allows me justification for not having to try new activities that I might feel anxious about, such as mingling at a social gathering or developing communication skills so I can feel comfortable interacting with others. My shyness protects me from the anxiety and apprehension of learning new skills and then practicing them in a social environment.

Anger

With that in mind, let's look at each of the feelings listed at the beginning of this section, beginning with anger. Anger is often referred to as a secondary emotion. What that means is that in any given moment when a person is feeling angry, their actual core or central emotion isn't necessarily one of anger, even though that may be all they and those around them are conscious of experiencing.

Instead, a more central emotion is driving the person, and feeling the anger helps the person stay out of the feeling that may be more painful. Usually, that primary emotion is fear, grief, loss, sadness, or some other emotion connected to a sense of not having enough or to a fear of impending deprivation. Anger protects the person from feeling that sense of deprivation.

Let's say I expect you to meet me as planned at 6:00 p.m. at my house. You don't show up or call, and when I see you on the following day I am angry about what happened. Here anger is the outward expression of my feeling that you shouldn't have treated me so inconsiderately by not calling to cancel. My expression of anger is an appropriate way to convey what behaviors are not acceptable to me and to inform others that I believe that I am entitled to respectful, considerate treatment.

However, my anger also shields me and others from my underlying, deeper feelings. I can access those deeper feelings by asking myself, "If I wasn't feeling anger right now, what else would I be feeling?" Probably I would be feeling hurt and afraid that I wasn't important enough to you for you to want to call. Or I might have been feeling worried that your life seems to be going in a different direction from mine, and I might have feared that we're growing apart.

My anger pulls me up out of those painful feelings to feel self-righteous, indignant, and able to shake my finger at you and say, "You're a bad person." Anger keeps me from being immobilized in my sadness and fear. Although that's sometimes useful, anger eventually takes its toll because it eats away at people both emotionally and physically.

> One way to begin switching to positive energy is to ask yourself, "What motivates me, what inspires or recharges me?"

Anger does have some useful purposes. One is to get people's attention and to let them know that their behavior is unacceptable. Suppose I counted on someone to pick me up at my doctor's office and the person never arrived. My anger would let my friend know that it's unacceptable to leave me stranded. Anger can be an indicator that you are somehow not currently able to live in alignment with your values. Your anger may be a sign that some significant part of your life violates some of your core values. This incongruence often creates ongoing feelings of anger because of the friction and dissonance created by attempting to resolve this internal and external contradiction. Anger can also serve as motivation and as a powerful source of energy. Suppose my best friend's partner decides to end the relationship and leaves her and their two small children. She can sit in a puddle of grief for the first three weeks after he is gone and feel as though she's falling apart, or she can pull herself up, be furious with him, and use her anger to fuel the necessary steps to care for herself and her children. The difficulty lies in learning not to run on that negative kind of energy and instead transfer over to a more positive energy.

One way to begin switching to positive energy is to ask yourself, "What motivates me, what inspires or recharges me?" Once you identify those things, you can use your inspirational or recharging images to motivate yourself. If being in beautiful surroundings inspires me, then I can focus on creating a life that includes enough money to make that a reality. That's a very different motivational force than focusing on showing your ex-partner how well you are doing with the intent of rubbing your ex-partner's nose in your success.

Guilt

It is important when thinking about guilt to separate the fact of guilt from the feeling of guilt. Sometimes we can be factually guilty, such as being guilty of failing to return a phone call when we promised we would. We can be guilty of not being sensitive to someone's feelings. Guilt in that sense serves as an internal smoke alarm to wake us up and make us aware of the fact that perhaps we have behaved in a way that does not align with our fundamental nature. It helps us realize that in some way we have violated our integrity or sense of how we choose to be in the world.

Guilt feelings, which are different than the fact of guilt, are ongoing, chronic, reemerging feelings that tend to be highly unproductive. They usually serve a number of purposes for the person feeling guilt. These purposes include controlling others ("Look how much you hurt me"); proving your good intentions ("I may have screwed up, but it's not because I didn't know what was right"); punishing yourself for how you failed ("I screwed up and deserve to suffer"); or sabotaging the positive things in your life ("I don't deserve to be happy").

How do you escape being stuck in guilt feelings? First, try to identify the purpose of your guilt feelings. If the purpose is to prove your good intentions, is there another way you could achieve that purpose without feeling guilt? You might consider doing something that demonstrates your good intentions, such as actually calling your friend rather than simply saying you feel guilty for not calling. When you say you feel guilty without fixing the situation with behavior that supports your words, in effect you ask to be forgiven for noticing you did something hurtful rather than taking action to heal the hurt.

Self-Doubt

What is self-doubt? Self-doubt is a lack of self-trust. It's when you overdo healthy self-questioning to the point where you no longer question what is so but rather your own judgment. You may lack trust in your ability to perceive things correctly; to make good, clear, healthy decisions; or to be able to understand a person or an opportunity and take appropriate action. You may constantly undermine yourself by wondering, "Is this right or is that right?" Ask yourself how important it is for you to do things perfectly; many people who get mired in self-doubt really are invested in doing everything right.

Part of what can interfere with your ability to move through the world with more confidence and certainty is the fact that often you may feel as though it's not permissible to make a mistake. You may constantly question, scan, and attempt to determine if you're behaving in ways that will allow you to do things well, thoroughly, or perhaps even perfectly.

Avoid basing your ability to trust yourself on whether all of your decisions have turned out well.

If this description sounds like you, consider attempting to free yourself from the trap of perfectionism. One way to begin this process is to decide in what area of your life you would be willing to be imperfect. That might mean having one messy dresser drawer or admitting you don't know something. The objective is to gradually free yourself of the burden of attempting to be or to appear to be perfect.

Self-doubt can also stem from previous life experiences in which you made the best choices you knew how to make at the time, but nonetheless the choices you made resulted in pain and loss. You may now be leery of making new choices and may doubt your ability to make even the simplest decision well. Start small with low-risk decisions, and give yourself permission to simply decide and to not have to decide perfectly. Avoid basing your ability to trust yourself on whether all of your decisions have turned out well. Sometimes they will, and sometimes they won't. Nevertheless, you can still trust yourself.

Anxiety

Anxiety is a response to stress or perceived danger. It comes out of basic biological programming to ensure physical survival. Anxiety is the sense of impending danger, the feeling that you need to be very careful or something bad will happen. It's designed to get your body into a state of readiness for either flight or fight, to get your body chemicals going so that you're able to take appropriate action in the face of danger.

Anxiety creates a problem when, instead of legitimately being in physical danger, you perceive yourself to be in emotional danger. Your body will still respond with the same anxiety response—pounding heart, accelerated breathing, and other physical symptoms. Although this may be helpful if we need either to physically fight or to flee, it is not helpful in an emotional context, such as giving a speech in front of a group. In that case, since you don't need to fight or flee, your anxiety is actually counterproductive. You may feel emotionally at risk because you feel uncertain whether the audience will respond positively to you, but your anxiety and physical response often hinder your ability to concentrate.

Besides being a physical state, anxiety is the feeling that often comes out of worrying or obsessing. One way to minimize your anxiety is to tell yourself that 98 percent of everything that you worry about or feel anxious about will never occur, and worrying won't positively change the other 2 percent. You might as well save your time and energy for dealing with the outcomes of situations rather than anxiously churning around inside.

Another way of coping with anxiety is to try to keep it from leaking out all over you throughout the day. Some people set aside regular, daily "worry time." To begin, they designate one half hour in the evening, after the house is quiet and everyone's in bed, when they will sit down and worry as hard as they can about everything they have to worry about.

In order for this to work, if you catch yourself worrying or obsessing about something over the course of the day, instead of thinking about it you just scribble a brief note so you'll remember to worry about it in the evening; then you continue with your day. When the evening worry time arrives, you pull out your notes and worry about all of those things.

One of two things usually happens when people do this. One is that they consolidate their worry and anxiety into a half hour in the evening; it doesn't permeate every waking moment, and therefore it's more effective and much more contained. Some people find that trying to worry for a half hour and think about nothing but worrying is boring; these people often say, "This is boring; I don't want to worry anymore," thereby helping to break the worry cycle. Either response is useful for dealing with chronic worrying.

Another useful technique is to ask yourself what you would be doing if you weren't worrying. Worrying often shields you from having to deal with other tasks, situations, and emotions that you'd rather not face. If you can identify what you're avoiding and give yourself permission to avoid dealing with it temporarily, you may alleviate much of your tendency to worry.

Depression

Depression is something most of us have felt to one degree or another at some point in our lives. It's that feeling of emotional heaviness, the feeling that everything that used to have a point no longer does, that things seem meaningless, pointless, and senseless. Usually it's hard to get up and move around, or else you feel restless so that it's hard to settle down. Nothing seems to satisfy or soothe you. There is a sense of emptiness, hopelessness, lack, and longing.

Depression usually stems from how you view things: is life all bad with bits of good, or is it just the opposite—is life usually positive with intermittent negative experiences? Your chances of experiencing depression depend on how you view life.

Depression is power and anger turned on the self, feeling and energy trapped with nowhere to go but inside.

Picture a big, expansive blue sky with small, fluffy white clouds floating across it. If you see life as good, you would see life represented by the blue sky with the clouds representing the bad things that occasionally obscure your positive experiences. Even when the sky is covered by clouds, you know that the good things in life are still there, that you will experience happy moments again.

However, if you see the clouds as random moments of good and the sky as the enduring bad experience of your life, you will find it difficult to enjoy positive experiences when they occur. Even when clouds cover the sky and your life looks good, you will think that behind it lurks this unending, irreversible bad stuff that's just waiting to happen, as soon as the clouds and the good moments pass by.

Depression is also about trapped power and unexpressed emotion. Depression is power and anger turned on the self, feeling and energy trapped with nowhere to go but inside. Once trapped inside it becomes toxic.

Often strong, true, clean emotions—anger, desire, loss—cannot be expressed in your current situation, and instead those emotions become stuck inside. What started out as fresh, pure, clean emotion is now trapped like water in a rain barrel—stale, musty, and toxic.

Trapped power is about not being able to express your individuality, your passions, and your desires; about not being able to make an impact, to be seen, heard, or acknowledged. It's about emotions that have nowhere to go but back inside. It's about living an existence in which either you are too fearful or your situation is too dangerous to allow you to feel and express your entire range of feelings. Eventually, the sense of hopelessness and ineffectiveness continues to grow, and the self slowly gives up and shuts down.

There are things you can do to move out of depression. First, find some small piece of power to claim for yourself, something small you can do to empower yourself. It could be as simple as organizing your sock drawer; or it might be to get up when you don't feel like it and walk four blocks—whatever it takes to help you experience a little power, feel something in your center, or feel even the smallest hint of aliveness. Each day, build on that; add another activity that helps you move or take charge over a small piece of your life. Another approach you can take is to list everything that you feel you cannot say or do, everything that you feel hopeless about. With a good friend or a counselor, look at what small pieces of your list you could start to tackle.

Depression is also about unexpressed loss and grief. It's about feeling that you can't protect and save all of the things that are important to you. It's about wanting to be more effective, to change your experience, yet feeling like you don't have the will or the power to do that. Look at what you wanted to change but couldn't; or look at what things you didn't want to change but couldn't prevent from changing. If your depression seems connected to current or past losses, you may want to read Chapter Three again for help in handling grief.

SELF-DEFEATING BEHAVIORS

In looking at how self-defeating behaviors can affect your life, it is important to explore the purposes of feelings, both in terms of how they pertain to emotions in general and specifically how they relate to self-defeating behaviors. You may be thinking, "I just have feelings—what does the 'purpose of feelings' mean?" You may believe that feelings happen inside of you and that they're just there.

Feelings do have purpose. Feelings either help you face or help you avoid facing certain situations or issues in your life. Imagine that someone is trying to give you feedback on the impact of your behavior and you respond to that feedback by getting angry. Your anger protects you from having to listen to and consider what the person has to say.

Self-defeating behaviors also serve purposes. Suppose a self-defeating behavior like procrastination helps you avoid facing your big perfectionist streak. Usually you're so immobilized by your desire to be perfect that you put things off until the very last minute. Then, even if you manage to get them done on time, you still have an excuse if your task doesn't turn out perfectly. You can say, 'Well, if I had more time I could have done it exactly right." Procrastination protects you from having to make your best effort and realizing that it might not be perfect.

So exactly what are self-defeating behaviors? Self-defeating behaviors sap up your energy, focus, and strength. They keep you from expressing, pursuing, and achieving what you want in your life. In addition, they often distract you from your real issues.

Picture a woman who was sexually abused as a child or who feels powerless in her current relationship. Imagine that she goes out and uses her credit cards to charge things that she can't afford to pay for. Then, rather than putting energy into healing her experience of being sexually abused, she focuses instead on the chaos and crisis created by her overspending. Any kind of disruptive behavior that derails her life and makes it more difficult to work on her real issues is a self-defeating behavior.

Figure 4.1

Self-defeating behaviors take your focus off moving toward your goals.

In addition, since she hasn't worked through her real issues, she is impaired in her ability to have productive, healthy intimate relationships. And because her partnership isn't the way she wishes it was, rather than openly express her hurt, fear, pain, and anger, she chooses to funnel all those feelings into shopping and creating arguments about finances rather than the real issue.

I think of self-defeating behaviors as the equivalent of chopping holes in your rowboat. Picture yourself rowing across a lake headed for the far shore. Self-defeating behavior is like stopping in the middle of the lake, picking up an ax, and chopping a hole in the bottom of your boat. You spend your time and energy bailing water out of your boat, trying to stay afloat, instead of rowing your way across the lake. All your energy and focus goes into bailing the water out—water that wouldn't be in the boat if you hadn't chopped those holes.

So, how can you eliminate a self-defeating behavior? First, you need to identify what your self-defeating behavior is and how it interferes with the smooth functioning of your life. Once you've identified the behavior, spend several days asking yourself and others what you lose by engaging in that behavior.

The next step is to focus on how you disown your responsibility for creating and maintaining your self-defeating behavior. You may find that you blame automatic responses, inherited genes, or other people for the existence of the behavior. If your self-defeating behavior is overeating and you are overweight as a result, you might blame your overeating on (1) not thinking about how much you are eating until after the food is gone; (2) inheriting big fat cells and a slow metabolism; (3) others making you feel emotionally empty so that you need to eat that much; or (4) just a big appetite.

Your next step in eliminating your self-defeating behavior is to fully own the fact that you engage in that behavior; no one and no thing makes you do it; and you are the only one who can stop the behavior. You can help yourself own your self-defeating behavior by saying, "I create the _____ (overweight, financial difficulties, feelings of inferiority) in myself and in my life." Then determine what small step you would be willing to take to move yourself from a victim stance, where your self-defeating behavior has control over you, to a stance of personal responsibility and power, where you take clear, definite action to change your life. Your first step might be to delay engaging in your self-defeating behavior by writing down your feelings or calling a friend before starting the behavior. Once you have identified the feelings that lead to your self-defeating behavior, you can consider options for addressing those feelings.

The concept of taking personal responsibility and power for eliminating the undesirable aspects of your life and for creating desirable elements is the main point of this book and the key to successfully navigating your life transition. You can either choose to be the active author of your own life, shaping and changing outcomes, or refuse to pick up the pen and, instead, let others write your story through their choices and decisions.

You can believe either that outside life events control the details and direction of your life or that *you* largely control your life through choices you make and fail to make. Even when events occur outside your control, do not take a victim stance of "poor, pitiful, powerless me." Instead, look for ways to regain a sense of power and control in your life.

Even when you cannot change things back to their pretransition state, you still have the power to shape and determine what you want to create next in your life. I encourage you to approach each emotional rock in a manner that allows you to ask, "How do I manage the _____ (fear, uncertainty, grief) present in my life in a way that maximizes my sense of power and control over the details and direction of my life?" Remember, you're only a victim as long as you continue to think you are. Once you act to regain control and power over your life, you move out of being a victim and into being the creator of your life.

COPING STRATEGIES

What are coping strategies and why are they important? In times of emotional pain or during major life transitions, when fear, loss, grief, and insecurity overtake you as you're trying to climb to the top of the transition cliff, it's essential that you have some way to soothe and nurture yourself. By that I mean the ability to comfort yourself without addiction, numbness, or damage to yourself or others. Most of us have grown up without much of a model of what it means to soothe ourselves. If we were fortunate, perhaps we had parents who knew how to comfort and soothe us. If you did, you can probably draw on some of your childhood experiences and use those in ways appropriate to your adult self now. However, most people don't recall feeling especially comforted or soothed in their pain.

An important part of developing coping strategies is discovering what truly comforts you. For many people, it's receiving comfort from someone else. If that's an option for you and there are supportive people in your life, that's wonderful. The best approach is often to say to those people, "I'm really not doing very well right now, and what I could really use, if it works for you, is to have someone come over and spend time with me."

It's important to develop a repertoire of comforting or coping skills.

If you don't have people like that in your life, and even if you do, you need to know how to generate comfort for yourself. Think about what you could do for yourself that would make you feel better—taking a hot bath, putting on some relaxing music, having a good meal, renting a video, reading a novel in bed, or having a good cry. It will take some experimenting to find what works for you. Some things will not work as well as others, and some things will work only sometimes.

It's important to develop a repertoire of comforting or coping skills. Try to stay away from anything with addictive properties—especially alcohol, drugs, gambling, eating, and shopping—because while they may distract you momentarily from your pain, they usually create greater pain down the road. I'm not saying don't have a pint of ice cream if that's an occasional thing you want to do. However, examine whether you are trying to cope in only one primary way that's going to result in more pain in the future.

If people are stuck in terms of thinking of comfort and coping strategies, sometimes I suggest that they ask other people what they do when they feel bad. Lots of times others have good ideas, or their ideas will trigger other ideas for you.

You might also think about what you would do for a kid who felt very bad in the same way you're feeling bad. Often the part of us that feels the worst is the child part. This child part feels that whatever you're going through will last forever; it can't look at things with a reasonable, rational, adult perspective to know that bad things are time-limited. Your child self needs comforting, soothing words and safe, reassuring gestures that convey that things will truly get better.

COMMUNICATING YOUR FEELINGS

Communicating your feelings involves being able to honestly, openly, directly, succinctly, simply, and clearly express and share your feelings without blame, shame, or finger-pointing, accusatory words. It's about being able to say directly how you feel, what you want, and what you think without having to be indirect or having to downplay your feelings by saying, "Well, I know this is probably really stupid, but . . ." Communication is being able to look at the other person clearly and calmly and say, "This is what matters to me, this is what I'm worried about, this is what I'd like to know." It's about noticing and naming what's true for you in terms of what you feel inside, in terms of your desires, worries, hopes, and longings.

Communicating feelings is one of the cornerstones of any relationship. If one or both partners in an intimate relationship, a friendship, or a coworker relationship can't express feelings in appropriate, clear ways, the relationship is going to experience a lot of painful, difficult times. Clear and appropriate communication is direct: vague terms, words, and expressions aren't used, and when one person asks for clarification, the other person is able and willing to provide it. Appropriate communication excludes screaming, throwing of objects, name calling, and demeaning, threatening, and dangerous behavior.

Many people use an "I message" as a model for communicating their feelings. An "I message" states "I feel . . ." and then talks about the person's feelings. In this form of communication, the speaker owns and takes responsibility for her feelings and does not try to place that responsibility on others. Saying "I feel angry" is very different from saying "You make me angry," which blames the other person for the feeling and assumes that person has the power to create the feeling.

One of the most vivid representations of the fact that we create our own feelings is an example that was shared with me in one of my counseling classes. Imagine that you're riding on a crowded city bus and you're standing up, holding on to the overhead bar. The bus suddenly stops, and the person behind you slams into your lower back, causing some pain.

You wait a moment for an apology or an excuse, but none comes, and you start to become angry. You think, "What a rude person." You get all worked up to turn around and scold the person; but when you do turn around, you see an elderly man struggling to maintain his balance while holding a load of packages.

Immediately, your anger melts away, and you feel a sense of compassion and concern for the fact that he is standing up because no one has offered him a seat. Your lower back still hurts as badly as it did in your moment of anger. What has changed, however, besides your emotions, is what you have told yourself about the situation. In the moment of anger, you were telling yourself that people shouldn't be that rude—they should apologize. In the moment of compassion, you were telling yourself that this person is trying to manage standing up and he's doing his best; you were feeling empathy for his situation. The blow to your lower back didn't create the feeling; rather, it's what you told yourself about the blow that created the emotion.

In much the same way, another person can't make you angry—it's what you tell yourself about their behavior that creates your angry feelings. Similarly, another person can't make you sad or joyful—it's what you tell yourself about your experiences that creates those emotions.

An I message states,

I feel   _____

when you   _____

because   _____

For each situation you can fill in the blanks with the appropriate words describing your feelings and thoughts. For instance, you can say,

I feel	*hurt and angry*
when you	*don't call when you're going to be late*
because	*i worry that you don't love me.*

That's different from saying, "You thoughtless, rude jerk, how come you never call me?"

Communicating your feelings requires a sense of timing. When someone walks in the door exhausted after a long day, regardless of how valid and important your feelings are, this may not be the best time to deliver those feelings. It's important to wait for a moment when someone is receptive and able to listen. If someone is never receptive, you should reexamine your relationship.

Also, pay attention to nonverbal communication, to what you're doing with your body, the tone of your voice, and the expression on your face. All of those things can contradict your verbal expression. Communication is more than getting the words right; it's choosing to communicate well rather than try to prove that you're right.

Many things can contribute to your communication going well. One key component in this process is making a sound decision regarding what and to whom to communicate. Ask yourself: What is appropriate to the situation and the person involved? How much information is pertinent to the situation? What kind of information does this person most need from me? What is my intention in communicating this? Is my intention muddy or clear? Do I want my communication to deepen understanding and connection or do I have a less positive intention underlying my words? Knowing your honest answers to these questions affords you the opportunity to communicate in a clear and direct manner, free of mixed messages and unnecessary confusion.

Another way to increase the likelihood of successful communication is to remember that people bring three primary questions to their interactions with others. These questions are usually unspoken and merely implied, although someone may voice one or more directly. The questions are: Am I safe? Do you like me? Do you understand me?

Many people carry these questions outside their conscious awareness, yet aren't fully able to give their full attention to the content of your communication until they have received positive answers to each of these questions. This doesn't mean that you answer the questions directly, rather it means finding ways to convey that the person is safe, understood, and liked by you in a way that meshes with your personal style. Doing this will allow the other person to relax and increase the possibility that your feelings and thoughts are well heard.

ASSERTIVENESS

Assertiveness is the ability to communicate your preferences, ideas, and feelings in a manner that is clear and direct. Assertiveness lets other people know, in essence, who you are as a person and what is important to you.

During times of transition, assertiveness is especially crucial because what you're used to doing and having present in your life suddenly changes. The connection and contact you need from people in your life may be radically different from what worked before the transition. Because many parts of your life are changing, you need to be assertive to define new boundaries and preferences.

Assertiveness helps define your limits and preferences. It says, "This is the person that I am, and I am defined by these things." It makes you visible to the world. It shows other people what is and is not okay with you.

In being assertive, you have to believe that it's worth having others momentarily displeased with you in order to get what is important to you.

It is difficult to be assertive if you have low self-esteem. If you don't believe you are worthy of having others behave appropriately toward you, or if you believe that it will be too much trouble or bother to ask people to do things for you, then it will be hard to be assertive. If you don't have much self-esteem, you may feel that it is selfish or wrong for you to want what you want, that you shouldn't rock the boat, that you should just go along with things, that it's easier and better that way. If this is true for you, pay attention to the following chapter, where you can work on increasing your self-esteem.

In being assertive, you have to believe that it's worth having others momentarily displeased with you in order to get what is important to you. I think one of the toughest things about assertiveness is that many of us assume that if we do it well, people will feel fine about us—they won't feel

Figure 4.2

Without assertiveness, it's difficult to set limits on how others treat you.

hurt or angry. We may also think that if we don't know how to be assertive so that people remain happy with us, then we shouldn't be assertive.

One of the key points about being assertive is that the receiver of the assertive message is almost always displeased about receiving that message. No one likes to be told "no" or have limits or boundaries set. People want what they want on their terms, and when you're assertive in saying "No, that's not okay with me," people tend to get upset and angry, possibly with the idea that their anger will cause you to back down and change your mind. An important part of being assertive is saying, "This is important to me and I'm willing to endure this person's displeasure for the moment."

When you're being assertive, ask for a behavior change, not an attitude change. Suppose you want to be assertive about expressing that you want more close, intimate talk with your partner. You want to talk about feelings and important emotions in the relationship. Asking for an attitude change, which is what you don't want to do, is saying, "I want you to love and value me more by talking to me about your feelings." The person who receives this message doesn't really know in specific behavioral terms what it would look like for you to get what you want.

What you want to do in making an assertive statement is to make an "I want" or an "I would like" statement that tells the person in behavioral terms what you would like. In this case, you might say, "I would like us to spend a half hour every night talking about how we're feeling about each other and the relationship or sharing some personal feelings about what is going on for us."

The recipient of this message still may not like your assertive request, but at least he knows what you are asking and can say, "A half hour every night is too much for me; how would every other night be?" Then negotiation can occur.

Being assertive doesn't have to be an all-or-nothing stance, especially in setting limits with others. You can set partial limits with people—for instance, "I can only talk with you for ten minutes on the phone tonight" rather than saying you can't talk at all. Your limits can be flexible; you can say that when you're rested and feeling good, you're happy to have people drop over to visit, but when you're stressed you want people to call first.

And remember, assertiveness isn't just about saying no and setting limits, it's also about saying yes to people and experiences—asserting your approval, your appreciation, your desire for more of what you enjoy. Being assertive can be about inviting others into your life, about letting them know what they do well, what you like about them. And the combination of knowing how to express your feelings and be assertive is amazingly impactful. Once you learn how to appropriately assert your truth, you have found your power. And once you have found your power, you have found your authentic self.

Here are some exercises that will help you begin to personalize the information presented in this chapter. Begin by writing yourself a prescription for self-awareness.

℞ FOR SELF-AWARENESS

1. I experience anger when

   ....

   ....

2. Situations in which I feel self-doubt include

   ....

   ....

3. Guilt arises for me when

_____

_____

4. I experience feelings of anxiety when

_____

_____

5. When I felt depressed in the past it was because

_____

_____

6. Some self-defeating behaviors I have engaged in are

_____

_____

7. The issues that engaging in these behaviors protected me from dealing with are

_____

_____

8. Some things that comfort me are

_____

_____

9. The feelings that I find easiest to communicate are

_____

_____

10. The feelings that I find hardest to communicate are

_____

_____

11. What I would most like to be assertive about is

_____

_____

FOR YOUR JOURNAL . . .

1. What did you learn about yourself from this chapter?
2. How does that change things for you or help you make sense of your life?
3. What else do you want to know about yourself?

RECOMMENDED READINGS

Burns, David. 1990. *Feeling Good Handbook.* New York: Penguin.

Provides useful information to help overcome fear, anxiety, procrastination, conflict, and self-defeating attitudes.

Clancy, Jo. 1997. *Anger and Relapse: Breaking the Cycle.* Psychosocial Press.

Explores reactions and responses to anger-inducing stituations and suggests ways to turn down your anger thermostat and balance your boundaries.

Cudnen, Milton and Hardy, Robert. 1993. *Self-Defeating Behaviors: Free Yourself from Habits, Compulsions, Feelings and Attitudes that Hold You Back.* New York: Harper.

Describes useful techniques for eliminating self-defeating behaviors.

Handy, Robert and Neff, Pauline 1985. *Anxiety and Panic Attack.* New York: Fawcett Crest.

Offers a straightforward step-by-step approach to reduce stress, anxiety, and painc attacks.

Lounden, Jennifer. 1992. *The Woman's Comfort Book.* San Francisco: HarperCollins.

Teaches you how to nurture yourself with over 200 suggestions of ways to comfort yourself, plus a quick "comfort at a glance" chart that matches feelings with specific comfort ideas.

Tavris, Carol. 1989. *Anger.* New York: Simon and Schuster.

Examines current research findings as well as the myths regarding the anatomy of anger, the expression of anger, and how anger affects people's lives.

SELF-ESTEEM AND SELF-PERCEPTION

DEFINING SELF-ESTEEM

Self-esteem is the ability to like yourself regardless of the feedback you receive from others—regardless of whether people approve of you, agree with you, or see things eye-to-eye with you. It is the ability to enjoy and appreciate all of yourself: the strengths that you are proud of as well as the shortcomings you are aware of, the gaps between what you know how to do and what you want to be able to do.

Self-esteem is being able to see yourself as worthy of love, attention, affection, respect, caring, and consideration. It is viewing yourself as worthy of those things even when you don't live up to your expectations or the expectations of others. It is being able to believe in your inherent value regardless of your performance, achievement, behavior, how much you do for others, or the current circumstances you are in. Self-esteem is being at peace with the knowledge of the importance of your existence.

The essence of self-esteem is the ability to remember that you are fundamentally enough no matter what others believe, say, or do. While people with healthy self-esteem are aware of the need to grow and challenge themselves in certain areas, they do not judge themselves harshly, nor do they believe that they need to be "fixed" before they are worthy of respect, kindness, consideration, or love. Because they value themselves, they are able to recognize poor relationships when others do not, and they take action to either change the relationships or remove themselves from them.

Self-esteem exists on a spectrum. No one has absolutely no self-esteem and no one couldn't use a little more self-esteem. You may know someone who seems to possess too much self-esteem. Very likely, this person continually proclaims how wonderful he or she is to anyone who will listen. This kind of behavior has nothing to do with high self-esteem. Rather, the need to prove one's worth to others is a sure indicator that the person is in doubt about his or her worth.

Your self-esteem will not be and does not need to be equally high in all aspects of your life. You may feel self-esteem in certain areas of your life and not in others. The growth process in self-esteem is similar to adolescent physical growth. Not every part of a teenager grows at an equal pace—feet and hands may grow to full size while height may lag behind. And just as a physical body need not be perfectly in proportion to be healthy and function well, your self-esteem need not be perfectly equivalent in all areas of your life in order for your sense of self-worth to be sturdy and well-established. And it is crucial that you see your baseline worth—the worth that exists regardless of whether or not you achieve or whether you comb your hair that day. Whether or not you have worth is not the issue, because you do have worth. The issue is whether or not you can feel and acknowledge your worth.

So what can you do if you notice that your self-esteem is lagging in certain aspects of your life? There are several approaches you can take to improve your self-esteem. A self-esteem assessment allows you to acknowledge your strengths and also focus on filling in your gaps. I've included as an example the exercise that I use myself, but feel free to alter it to reflect what is pertinent for you or to construct your own from scratch.

What are the best things about me?

Things that others know	*Things that only I know*
1. _____	1. _____
2. _____	2. _____
3. _____	3. _____

What are my shortcomings?

Things that others know	*Things that only I know*
1. _____	1. _____
2. _____	2. _____
3. _____	3. _____

Make your lists as long or as short as you wish. Put a plus by the aspects you feel fine about. Put a star by the things you want to change.

What is a realistic, healthy level of change for each item you put a star by? Remember to be reasonable, not perfectionist in your goals.

 Pick one item you want to start changing now. What small step could you take this week that would put you on your way to changing it? Each completed small step will make the next step more exciting as you see yourself grow and change.

Another approach to increasing your self-esteem is what I call the "loving foster parent." Since the foundations for self-esteem are built or damaged during childhood, this approach focuses on the source of those early feelings and decisions about your self-worth.

 Imaginge that you've been asked to take care of a young foster child. The caseworker has shared the child's self-esteem issues with you, and now that the caseworker has left, you are standing looking at the child. Now imagine that the child has the same self-esteem issues you currently have. What would you do to help the child start to build her self-esteem? How would you treat the child? What things would you want to say to help her heal and begin to feel better about herself?

Your responses to the above questions will provide clues to how you can fortify your own sense of self-esteem. You can begin saying and doing for yourself the same things that you would do for a small child, or you can enlist the assistance of a supportive friend or partner to provide some of those behaviors or words. Anything that helps you feel valued and appreciated for who you are right now will help increase and strengthen your self-esteem. And any self-esteem you can develop will help create sturdy handholds to help you climb to the top of the transition cliff.

Another excellent way to build your self-esteem is by consciously choosing to be real—letting people see the genuine you and trusting that while some may not care for the real you, those who like you will actually be liking the true you. It's hard to feel the self-esteem that can come from being liked and valued when you're being valued for traits or behaviors that aren't a genuine part of who you are. You can also build your self-esteem by keeping your word, by following through on what you promise or agree to, by being accountable for your words and actions, and by feeling the self-esteem that comes from living your life from a place of integrity. And remember, the confidence will come from doing, which in turn will lead to the confidence to simply be.

SELF-PERCEPTION VS. THE PERCEPTION OF OTHERS

Self-perception consists of the attitudes, beliefs, and feelings you have about yourself. One important aspect of self-perception is its consistency or stability—does your self-perception remain constant and stable or does it fluctuate?

Q Is your self-perception largely independent of the perceptions of others or is it shaped by them?

A _____

_____

_____

Can you view yourself accurately as you are in reality or is your vision of yourself clouded by belief systems passed to you by your family or others?

_____

_____

_____

Self-perception is how you view and assess yourself in relation to your expectations and those of others. The clearer the distinction between your self-perception and the perception of others, the less likely you are to be knocked off balance by someone's inaccurate negative perception—and the better equipped you will be to respond to feedback with openness and objectivity.

Self-perception relates to self-esteem in that how we perceive ourselves and how we allow others' perceptions to affect us can have a substantial impact on our self-esteem. If I am capable of perceiving myself accurately, that will contribute to my self-esteem in two ways:

1. I will be able to see my strengths, accomplishments, and qualities clearly, own them, and consciously carry that knowledge around with me.

Figure 5.1

Walt's self-perception is based on the view of others.

2. I will also be able to devote my energy to filling in the gaps in my knowledge and abilities, increasing my sense of mastery and self-growth.

However, if my self-perception isn't accurate and I can't see my strengths and shortcomings, I may not have the clarity to take action, thus feeling worse about myself and contributing to a lower sense of self-esteem.

While I may enjoy the approval of others, it is important that I don't require their approval to feel good about myself.

The perception of others factors into self-esteem in several ways. Everyone likes approval from others. To say that the ultimate goal is to be free of the desire to have others approve of us fails to take into consideration the fact that we are social beings, and that part of feeling bonded to others is a sense of their liking and approval.

This can cause difficulties if your self-esteem is contingent upon the approval of others. While I may enjoy the approval of others, it is important that I don't require their approval to feel good about myself. If I do, I can become dependent on their approval, and as a consequence, my self-esteem can fluctuate based on how much approval I get at the moment.

If you are aware that much of your self-esteem is based on the approval of others, what can you do to change it? You can start by picking one behavior you use largely to gain someone's approval. Each day, make a conscious effort not to use that behavior in at least one situation. Notice how you feel when you refrain from engaging in that behavior, and give yourself support and positive feedback. Continue to increase the frequency of not engaging in approval-seeking behavior as you become more accustomed to generating your own approval.

And what if you discover that you don't like yourself, regardless of the positive feedback that you receive from others? What if you feel like a fraud when people comment on your positive attributes, skills, and strengths? What if they see you as kind, thoughtful, and good, and you see just the opposite? Well, everyone I've ever met is at least a little good, kind, and thoughtful and at least a little mean, self-absorbed, and unkind in moments. We all have both sets of qualities in us. To believe we only have one set would be like insisting it's always nighttime when daylight comes every day. To have angry feelings, impulses, unkind thoughts, and the like does not make you bad, unworthy of love, or a fraud—it just makes you human.

INTERNAL VS. EXTERNAL LOCUS OF CONTROL

Locus of control refers to where you believe the control over your life is located: internally, within yourself; or externally, out in the world, putting you under the control of others.

External locus of control means that when something fortunate happens, rather than acknowledge and take credit for the role I played in creating the success, I instead attribute that success to luck, to being in the right place at the right time, or to others being kind to me.

External locus of control can also mean that when something unfortunate occurs, rather than accepting my role in creating it, I attribute my misfortune to a force outside myself, something that is outside my power and control to foresee, prevent, or minimize.

Internal locus of control is just the opposite. It means that when something positive occurs, I accept and acknowledge the part I played in creating it. And when something unfortunate occurs, I accept my part in its creation and look for the knowledge that I can gain to respond differently should the situation rise again.

Internal locus of control says that I have the ability to change my life in positive and negative ways, and even if sometimes I am unaware of exactly *how* to change it, I am always aware that I have that ability. I am also aware that as I gain more knowledge I can change or adjust how I respond to a situation.

External locus of control implies that I don't have the ability to shape my life because the impact of outside forces is so strong that they will inevitably determine the outcome. This sets up a fatalistic stance in which I think, "I'm not powerful enough, so I'm at the whim of outside forces and can be victimized by them."

This belief system often has its roots in early childhood experiences where you weren't powerful enough and were victimized. But as an adult, while your feelings might be the same, you *do* have the power to change your life.

Ways to Reclaim Your Power

Think of a current situation in which you would like to feel more powerful. Make a list of all the ways you could reclaim your power. As an example, let's assume you wish you had the power to cause your partner to be more committed in the relationship. Instead of feeling helpless and at the whim of your partner's feelings, you could reclaim your power.

* Make a commitment to yourself and your well-being by promising to be unendingly loyal to yourself and not dump your sense of well-being to try to win someone's love. You might even buy yourself a ring to formalize your commitment to yourself.
* Focus on what you *can* change: your attitude about yourself and others, your zest for life, your immediate physical environment, your work and sense of financial stability, and your relationships with others.

- Create a relationship timeline showing where you want the relationship to be in five years. Decide how long you are willing to remain in the relationship without receiving the commitment you want.

- Explore and build other options so that remaining in the relationship is a clear choice rather than a nondecision based on survival needs.

If you feel unable to generate ideas for how you could claim power in a certain situation, solicit input from others. They may suggest things that you wouldn't want to do, but write them down anyway. The purpose is to increase your awareness of options for regaining personal power, and considering an option does not obligate you to choose it.

SELF-TALK AND SELF-ACCEPTANCE

One big factor determining your level of self-esteem is the quality of the self-talk that goes on in your head. Most of us have an internal tape in our head that chatters at us as we go through our day—an internal "voice" that comments on our behavior.

Imagine that you are in a meeting with a group of people, and you make a suggestion that is met with blank looks and silence. Your self-talk is the internal dialogue that comments on your experience. Positive self-talk in this situation might sound like this: "Well, even though no one is responding, I think my idea is a good one, and I'll restate it in a manner that's easier for people to grasp." Negative self-talk would take the form of "That is the most stupid thing I have ever said—now everyone is going to know what an idiot I am." Positive self-talk maintains or increases your level of self-esteem, while negative self-talk chips away at whatever self-esteem you might have attained.

Another aspect of self-talk is that what you hear over and over again shapes your beliefs. So if you repeatedly hear "I'm doing fine, I believe in myself, I'm a good person, I'm making my best attempt," then over time that's what you start to believe. If you tell yourself, "I'm awful, I'm stupid, I'm ugly," then over time that is what you come to truly believe. This internal commentary has a powerful way of shaping how you feel about yourself.

Knowing how the quality of your self-talk affects your self-esteem, what can you do to make your self-talk more positive? One good way to do that is by creating and utilizing affirmations. An affirmation is a positive statement that expresses how you want to feel or be as if that were already true. For example: "I attract loving and giving people into my life" or "I handle new situations with grace, ease, and enthusiasm." The idea is to phrase your affirmation in the here and now and use feeling words. Do not state things in the future tense, such as "I will learn" or "Someday, I may feel happy." Instead, state it as if it is already happening: "I feel joyous" or "I am strong." Also do not use negative words such as "no," "never," "don't," or "can't." State your affirmations in positive terms such as "I am capable" rather than "I am not a screw-up." One straightforward, nearly universally useful affirmation is "I can do it."

Positive self-talk maintains or increases your level of self-esteem, while negative self-talk chips away at whatever self-esteem you might have attained.

You may doubt that creating positive statements about yourself can increase your self-esteem. The key to having affirmations work is to write them down and place them where you'll see them frequently. Say them out loud, because using your voice helps to further convince your mind that your affirmation is true. Finally, repetition is crucial. Your mind needs to see and hear your positive affirmations repeatedly in order to finally rid itself of negative self-talk and increase your self-acceptance. And even though it can sometimes seem that you truly should feel good about yourself before using affirmations to tell yourself positive things, just the opposite is true. As you continue to practice using positive affirmations, your self-esteem and self-acceptance will gradually start to improve.

How does self-acceptance relate to self-talk? Self-acceptance is the result of healthy self-talk. Replacing your internal negative voice with a positive voice is like having an internal supportive coach, mentor, or teacher cheering you on. In the beginning it often seems difficult to turn negative self-talk into positive self-talk. You may need to create a positive voice that you attribute to a higher authority to help shut out the negative voice. Think about your ideal supportive person. Would it be a wise mentor, a "kick in the seat of the pants" coach, a group of people led by someone cheering you on? Whatever is the most powerful image for you is what you want to internalize so that it can contradict and argue with your negative self-talk. It can be someone you know, someone imaginary with traits you wish someone supportive would have, or someone you know from public life.

My own internalized, self-accepting voice is James Earl Jones. I picked him because he has a deep, resonant, full-bodied, authoritative voice. When my self-talk starts attacking my self-esteem, I substitute his voice saying, "Nonsense, you did a splendid job." It helps minimize the negative voice in my head and gives me a positive belief to focus on. It is impossible to simply extinguish a behavior that you don't like without replacing it with another behavior. Just trying to eliminate negative self-talk without substituting anything in its place creates a void, and it is much easier for the negative self-talk to slip back in.

Self-acceptance helps you value, appreciate, and love yourself for what you are capable of right now.

Self-acceptance helps you value, appreciate, and love yourself for what you are capable of right now. It may not be all that you ever want to achieve or accomplish, it may not be up to the standards you ultimately want to reach, but it represents the best you are capable of at this point in time. Once you can accept yourself, it becomes much easier to move through the world with safety, comfort, and ease. It also becomes much easier to accept and value others without demanding perfection from them, thereby increasing the likelihood of creating healthy, loving relationships—a topic we'll explore in Chapter Six.

APPROVAL-SEEKING AND CODEPENDENCY ISSUES

Some of the biggest issues for the women whom I teach in the transitions program are approval-seeking and codependency issues. When your self-esteem is lower than you'd like and when you've been raised to look outside of yourself for your sense of self-worth, you are often caught in a vicious cycle of trying to win others' approval in order to feel better about yourself.

The problem is that the more you do this, the more you seem to need to do it. It can become an addictive cycle because if you can get someone else to like you, you can get a little relief from your feelings of low self-esteem. But because this relief comes from the outside:

1. You can't control its intensity or frequency.
2. You can't give it to yourself when you need it the most.
3. It is dependent upon your ability to win someone else's approval.

So rather than do what you feel is best for you or what is most in line with your integrity, you may express yourself in an unauthentic way in order to get a positive response. This could take the form of pretending to agree with beliefs or opinions when you actually do not.

Even if you get a positive response, you know you have behaved fraudulently in order to get approval. So even if approval temporarily relieves your low self-esteem, it also simultaneously diminishes your self-esteem if you know you have been dishonest about who you are or what you believe in order to get approval.

If you grew up in a dysfunctional family, you most likely were taught that your worth was conditional upon how much you pleased your caretakers. Those early lessons about the world are the hardest to overcome. It is no accident, then, if because you feel you need someone's approval, you can slip into behaving codependently toward that person.

Definitions of codependence abound in popular literature. My definition is *consistently choosing to value another person's existence and focusing on the details of that person's life at the expense of valuing your own existence and focusing upon your own well-being and personal growth.* Codependent behavior tries to control the other person in order to get the response you feel you need from that person to feel okay about yourself. Codependence can also occur when you get caught up in the lives of others in order to avoid dealing with your own issues and struggles.

Codependence has the following effects:

1. loss of energy to channel into your own pursuits because you are so focused on the other person
2. loss of appropriate self-involvement in your interests, abilities, and goals
3. loss of balance because, in stepping so far into someone else's life, you are not fully present in your own
4. a chaotic, drama-stricken, out-of-control life because you are trying to control and manage things you have no power over

5. a sense of being run ragged, stressed out, and overwhelmed from trying to manage the unmanageable

6. feelings of resentment because the person whose life you are attempting to manage isn't appreciative of your efforts

How do you break out of this habit if you notice that it is developing? One small step is to try to do one nice thing for yourself when you notice that you are behaving codependently. You redirect your energy from managing another person's life and instead read a book, soak in the tub, call a friend, or take a walk.

An additional small step is to ask yourself which of your own aspects or issues you could be focusing on right now if you weren't focusing on the other person. Try sending the responsibility of other people's behavior back to them, let them be accountable for their actions, and take responsibility for only your own behavior. Start by focusing on yourself rather than them for fifteen minutes, and gradually increase the length of time.

* *

Give yourself positive feedback even if you make a mistake.

* *

Another way to change this tendency is to turn your focus elsewhere. Let go of spending so much energy trying to shape and control how others think of you—your energy can be used in other more beneficial pursuits (and trying to control others' views never works anyway). Instead of focusing on other people and trying to make them sturdy, healthy, or happy so they can approve of you, place your focus on approving of and strengthening your sense of self. For instance, if you are at a gathering and you are not dressed like anyone else, instead of hoping for positive feedback from someone, stop your process at that moment and picture your focus on other people as a light beam. Turn that light beam to focus it back on yourself, asking, "Do I approve of what I'm wearing and do I like it?"

Give yourself positive feedback even if you make a mistake. It is a matter of giving yourself approval, if not for the outcome of your attempts then at the very least for the effort behind them. You can find many things to approve of about yourself, even if you are thinking, "I don't approve of anything." You can approve of:

* the effort or intent behind what you do
* your determination to figure things out
* the fact that your heart is still beating
* the authenticity of your feelings
* the awareness of your discomfort

You can always find something to approve of even if you don't like the full outcome.

Another way to avoid trying to get others to approve of you is to focus on approving of others instead. Look for things you genuinely appreciate about others and give feedback. It creates a situation of safety and goodwill, taking the painful, vigilant focus off yourself.

SETTING AND MAINTAINING BOUNDARIES

What exactly is a boundary? Boundaries can be physically or psychologically based. A physical boundary is determined by how much you want to allow or limit access to your physical self. A mental or emotional boundary is the psychological line you draw around yourself that says this is where you end and other people begin. How sturdy and definite your boundaries are depends on many factors. It largely depends on how much you were taught as a child that you had a right to your own separateness and distinctness, or how much you were expected to allow others access to your mental and emotional inner life.

Some families allow each member a great deal of psychological privacy and separateness. Other families function in an enmeshed environment, where individuals aren't allowed private thoughts and feelings, and everything is considered open. This can make functioning in the world a confusing and frightening process if you aren't certain how to set clear boundaries that others understand and respect.

Creating firm, clear boundaries is important because it helps you stay safe in the world and allows you to decide how much you want to let someone into your emotional space. I encountered a good description of boundary setting in a counselor training class, where an instructor represented boundary setting as the difference between having an internal versus an external zipper. Picture that you have a zipper running from beneath your chin down to your belly button. The zipper allows or denies access to your emotions. An external zipper has the pull tab on the outside of your body, while an internal zipper has the pull tab on the inside. With an external zipper, anyone you meet can potentially grab the

Figure 5.2

Alex suddenly realizes the importance of having her zipper pull tab on the inside.

pull tab and open it as far as they want, allowing themselves access to whatever amount of your private emotional life or personal details that they want. An internal zipper, on the other hand, allows you to control how much emotional access a person has to your feelings and thoughts. When you meet someone, you can decide how safe and trusting you feel and determine how far you want to lower your zipper and whether you want to let that individual in.

Many people have a preset level to which they automatically lower their zipper when they meet new people. It is their way of assuming that people are trustworthy until they prove otherwise, and also of making certain that they allow people access to only some of their emotional lives until they determine if they want to become more emotionally intimate.

Setting boundaries with people requires the assertiveness skills that you learned in Chapter Four. Part of what makes boundary setting so challenging is that no one likes to have limits placed on them or hear "No, you can't have access to that part of me." If you experience difficulties saying "no," continue to practice in small ways, remembering that you get good at what you practice.

Some relationships allow you to set boundaries in a relatively comfortable, easy way because that person's sense of boundaries will naturally mesh with your own. Others will have very different ideas about what is appropriate, and you may need to agree to disagree on your respective viewpoints. Despite someone's reaction, you never need to apologize for wanting to keep parts of your life private.

Maintaining boundaries is often even more difficult because many people want to test the limits, thinking that if you make an exception for them, it indicates their special status and importance. Let's say you told a friend not to call you between 5:00 and 7:00 P.M. because you are busy with the kids and dinner. You've set that boundary clearly; your friend adheres to it for a time, but eventually she starts calling during those hours. This is where you make a decision about what is the most important thing: Is your friend going through a difficult time and needing extra support from you, or do you need to reassert your boundaries?

> Setting and maintaining boundaries states that what you want, feel, and are comfortable with is important.

To maintain a boundary, reiterate your stand. If your boundary continues to be violated, state the consequences to the other person. Either the boundary is honored or you will spend less time with that person. Sometimes it may not be possible to continue even an important relationship with someone who refuses to respect your boundaries.

By not allowing others more access to your sense of self than you want, you also honor your own preferences and desires, which in itself is an act of self-esteem. People with low self-esteem have a difficult time believing that they are worthy enough to say no to other people. They believe that others are more important than they are, so how dare they say, "This part of me is important, and I'm keeping it private." Setting and maintaining boundaries states that what you want, feel, and are comfortable with is important, you choose to honor that, and you expect others to do the same. And if you'd like, you can visualize boundaries as the fence around the garden of your self-esteem, with your boundaries protecting all of the precious aspects that you've been cultivating and nurturing in your developing self-esteem.

Here are some exercises that will help you begin to personalize the information presented in this chapter. Begin by writing yourself a prescription for self-awareness.

R✕ FOR SELF-AWARENESS

1. Areas in my life where my self-esteem feels sturdy are

   _____

   _____

2. Areas in my life where I'd like my self-esteem to be stronger are

   _____

   _____

3. If I was to be fully real with others

   _____

   _____

4. When my words and actions match I feel

   _____

   _____

5. Approval that I want to receive from others includes

   _____

   _____

6. Things I have the power to impact are

   _____

   _____

7. Things I'd like to develop the power to impact are

   _____

   _____

8. An affirmation I'd like to try giving myself is

   _____

   _____

9. One way I focus on others instead of myself is

   _____

   _____

10. My fears about setting boundaries are

    ....

    ....

11. Setting boundaries could improve my life by

    ....

    ....

Feel free to renew your prescriptions periodically or rewrite them to accommodate your current needs and goals.

Prior to writing in your journal, complete the brag sheet exercise. Answer each section as proudly and completely as you can, and then respond to the questions for your journal.

BRAG SHEET EXERCISE

1. Three things that I do well:

    ....

    ....

    ....

2. Personal characteristics that I am proud of:

    ....

    ....

    ....

3. Three things that are best about me:

    ....

    ....

    ....

FOR YOUR JOURNAL . . .

1. What did you learn about yourself from this chapter?
2. How does that change things for you or help you make sense of your life?
3. What else do you want to know about yourself?

RECOMMENDED READINGS

Beattie, Melody. 1996. *Codependent No More*. San Francisco: HarperCollins.

Identifies the characteristics of codependency and teaches the basics of self-care as a means to begin recovering from codependency.

Bragg, Terry. 1997. *31 Days to High Self-Esteem: How to Change Your Life So You Have Joy, Bliss, and Abundance*. Peacemakers Training.

Explains a practical, step-by-step process for enhancing and enriching your self-esteem by taking responsibility for how you live your life.

Branden, Nathaniel. 1998. *How to Raise Your Self-Esteem*. New York: Bantam Doubleday Dell.

Provides step-by-step techniques for increasing self-esteem, including sentence completion exercises that encourage greater self-awareness.

Butler, Pamela. 1991. *Talking to Yourself*. San Francisco: HarperCollins.

Teaches ways to increase positive self-talk to reduce feelings of insecurity, depression, and poor self-image.

Cooper, Terry. 1996. *Accepting the Troll Underneath the Bridge: Overcoming Our Self-Doubts*. Mahwah, NJ: Paulist Press.

Uses a troll as a metaphor for the negaive, internal voice that can raise your deepest fear of inadequacy and provides useful tips for how to understand and deal with that internal voice.

Helmstetter, Shad. 1998. *The Self-Talk Solution*. New York: Simon and Schuster.

Teaches how to reprogram negative inner dialogues with motivating self-talk. Assists with increasing self-confidence and optimism.

McKay, Matthew and Fanning, Patrick. 1994. *Self-Esteem*. Oakland, CA: New Harbinger.

Provides detailed instructions indicating how to deal effectively with your internal critic, use visualization to increase your self-esteem, and develop more compassion toward yourself and others.

Minchinton, Jerry. 1993. *Maximum Self-Esteem*. Vanzant, MI: Arnford House.

Focuses on reducing the causes, rather than just the symptoms, of low self-esteem by learning to shed false beliefs and ceasing to dislike yourself.

INTERACTING
WITH OTHERS

HEALTHY AND DYSFUNCTIONAL RELATIONSHIPS

What is a healthy relationship? A healthy relationship is one in which your individuality is strengthened by your connection with another person. A healthy relationship allows room for you to grow; to express yourself; to have differing opinions; to be open, vulnerable, scared, affectionate, excited, and sad; and to be accepted as a worthwhile person regardless of whether someone is pleased with your behavior. In this kind of relationship, you are not asked to give up any integral part of yourself—your feelings, independent thoughts and beliefs, or your way of being in the world.

In healthy relationships, power is not used to dominate; rather, each person uses his or her own personal power and is able to do the things he or she deems important and valuable. In addition, each individual provides support and encouragement for the other person, doing what is possible and reasonable to help the other feel personally empowered.

A dysfunctional relationship is one in which aspects of the above are not possible. There may be bullying, intimidation, some form of abuse—verbal, emotional, physical, or sexual—or threats and coercion used to control the other person.

In a dysfunctional relationship there is room for only agreement, not individuality and differences. Your uniqueness is devalued; your worth is in question. You come out of interactions feeling less than you did going into them. These relationships consistently and chronically seem to suck out your life energy. They take your strengths and the best of you and belittle them, leaving you no room for growth, acceptance, love, or caring. In a dysfunctional relationship you are under siege, held hostage emotionally in a psychological war zone, never knowing when you're going to catch another piece of emotional shrapnel. You're diminished and devalued by the connection, and who you are as an individual is in danger because of the destructiveness of the relationship. There is no room to be freely yourself, to freely express yourself. Love is not possible because control, domination, and disruption take precedence over caring emotions.

* *

In a dysfunctional relationship there is room for only agreement, not individuality and differences.

* *

How do you know if a relationship is healthy or unhealthy? How do you determine whether a relationship merely has challenges, struggling points, and issues to be discussed, negotiated, and resolved—or is truly unhealthy and perhaps needs to be terminated?

One good gauge is to look at the level of respect and regard for one another that is present in the relationship. There can be massive disagreements about choices in career, how you spend your leisure time, finances, political issues, child-rearing concerns, what you find funny, choice of friends, choice of areas to live—and still a relationship can be healthy.

What allows substantial differences to exist within a healthy relationship is the level of respect accorded each person's individuality, preferences, opinions, beliefs, and choices. I don't need to agree with you or see things eye-to-eye in order to have a healthy relationship with you. I do need to respect you and not denigrate you for your differing opinions. In healthy relationships communication is always a possibility, even when it doesn't result in agreement. It might very well result in choosing to agree to disagree. In healthy relationships both partners are seen for who they are, for their uniqueness, and for their abilities and strengths. They are able to be heard for their values, opinions, preferences, wants, and joys, and acknowledged for the unique contributions they bring to the relationship.

Healthy relationships allow each partner to affect the other without damage. Healthy relationships exist on a continuum—what might feel healthy, satisfying, and appropriate for one person may be entirely different for another. Despite disagreement and disappointments, in healthy relationships no deep damage is done to a person's self-esteem, sense of self, dignity, or self-worth.

Unhealthy or dysfunctional relationships are just the opposite—in them the partners are not seen as who they truly are; they are not heard; their opinions are drowned out; someone is bullied into submission; dominance prevails; and blame, shame, and punitive behavior are the major forms of communication rather than acceptance, appreciation, and celebration of the other person.

In dysfunctional relationships each person feels diminished and less valued because of the connection; his or her human worth and dignity are in question. Rather than experiencing normal disagreements and disappointments, the partners feel damaged and deeply wounded by the interactions.

> What allows substantial differences to exist within a healthy relationship is the level of respect accorded each person's individuality, preferences, opinions, beliefs, and choices.

In my private psychology practice, individuals often ask me, "How come I seem to keep attracting or being attracted to partners who aren't good for me?" Part of what causes this is that we are drawn to situations that have components or familiar aspects of painful situations in our childhood that we did not have the power to change. In an effort to grow and attain mastery over events that we didn't have mastery over as children, in our adult life we unconsciously seek partners who embody at least some of the characteristics of important people who were the source of pain that we couldn't alleviate earlier in life.

Rather than being a source of doom ("Oh great, no matter what I do, I'm going to attract people who ignore me just as my father did"), this is actually a positive drive to solve what was unsolvable in childhood. Unfortunately, even if you do manage to pick a partner who exhibits that trait and even if you do manage to do things differently as an adult, this still won't heal that early childhood wound. The only way to really heal that childhood wound is to obtain personal counseling, write in a journal, join a support group, or do something that actually works at healing the initial wound. Trying to heal old wounds through your day-to-day adult life never seems to work.

Knowing this, how can you tell if you are attracted to someone as part of attempting to heal old wounds? What I often hear from individuals in my practice and women in the Transitions to Success program is that they don't realize that they have picked a partner with characteristics from their past until they are entrenched in the relationship.

One good way to try to spot this pattern early in a relationship is to examine your excitement level. A young woman in my practice was once talking about the young men in her life, whom she referred to as "boys." She was feeling a great deal of agony over one young man because he was distant, evasive, and did not call her when he said he would. She said, "But he's so exciting. I always feel like I'm living on the edge." So I said to her, "It sounds like he's an excitement boy." And she said, "That's it—he really is an excitement boy."

Then she went on to describe a female friend who had been dating a young man. The two women went over to watch videos at his house, and as the evening progressed they grew cold and hungry. The young man brought them blankets, bowls of macaroni and cheese, and big mugs of coffee; and as she finished relating the story, she said, "I didn't know there were boys out there that did the same things that I did for people, that like to care for other people." I said to her, "So he's a love boy, a boy who likes to nurture and love other people." So that became our code phrase for looking at her relationships—was her current date an excitement boy or a love boy?

The kind of person who loves you steadily and well probably isn't going to take you to never-ending peaks of ecstasy and pits of despair.

Part of what we learned together in exploring her choice of partners is that it is perfectly okay to pick an excitement partner if what you want is excitement and to live on the edge emotionally, feeling sweeping lows and soaring highs. All of that can be a wonderful adrenaline rush; just don't expect love partner behavior out of that person. An excitement partner probably isn't going to bring you a steaming bowl of macaroni and cheese or, upon learning you have a miserable cold, come over with chicken soup and videos.

So whatever you want to choose in the moment, choose it freely and enjoy it; but don't expect a love partner to be an excitement partner, and don't expect an excitement partner to be a love partner. The kind of person who loves you steadily and well probably isn't going to take you to never-ending peaks of ecstasy and pits of despair.

Part of what creates dysfunctional relationships is that someone looks at an excitement partner and believes it is possible to turn that person into a love partner. If you hang out with an excitement partner and just enjoy the excitement until it becomes hurtful or disruptive, you can have a lot of enjoyment. But what usually creates the excitement is that something about the excitement partner vaguely reminds you of some significant trait an important adult possessed—an adult who created childhood pain for you. Much of the excitement comes from the opportunity to grapple with the issue again, to struggle with a partner who is not accessible, who is preoccupied with other things, or who has a substance abuse problem. And while the partner might be entertaining for two weeks or two months, he probably isn't going to turn out to be a love partner anywhere in the near future. The person is not going to emerge as someone who can love you back with an equal and answering force.

It's perfectly acceptable to choose an excitement partner and enjoy the emotional rush. Just be conscious that you are doing it and don't get too attached to be able to let go when the relationship no longer works. If you don't feel ready to settle down with someone who loves you solidly and well, that's fine; just don't bemoan the fact that you can't turn an excitement partner into a love partner. They are two very different species, and while sometimes excitement partners grow into people who can nurture and love deeply, it's usually a gradual process that won't occur in the course of a brief relationship no matter how wonderful you are.

SEPARATENESS AND TOGETHERNESS

How much togetherness and separateness is right for you in your relationships? Do you find yourself disagreeing with others about how much time you are spending with them? What amount of alone time do you like? How much closeness do you want? The issue of separateness and togetherness is present in all relationships.

The need for separateness and togetherness is a relationship is crucial. As we begin to grow as infants and reach age two, one of the developmental tasks we grapple with and attempt to successfully complete is the tug between separateness and togetherness. Imagine a mother is sitting on the couch while her daughter, two-year-old Jenny, is sitting with her looking at a book. All of a sudden, Jenny gets tired of the closeness and wants to scamper down the hall and go exploring. So she heads down the hall, turns back to look at mom, gets an encouraging wave or smile, and continues down the hall.

Later, she realizes mom isn't within sight and she panics. Jenny then feels a strong need to reconnect, regardless of how much she has been enjoying her autonomy and independence. She rushes back down the hall to make certain that her mom is still sitting on the couch. She sees mom and feels relief. The process continues as Jenny realizes that she can connect, separate, and then reconnect without fear of disapproval or punishment.

That ability to move freely between moments of togetherness and moments of separateness is just as essential to our adult sense of well-being as it is to a two-year-old child. If our childhood caretakers were not equally comfortable with the competing needs of separateness and togetherness within themselves, they may not have been able to tolerate or facilitate our developing desires to connect and separate.

Sometimes we grow up polarized in one direction or another. A "people person" is typically comfortable only when together with other people; separateness makes that person anxious and restless. Or you might hear someone refer to herself as "a loner"; too much togetherness makes that person feel smothered and trapped. This polarization can occur as follows: If mom and dad weren't comfortable with their own independence or separateness, or if they had needs that weren't being met in adult relationships and needed us to be close to them, they may not have been sturdy enough to support our separateness. So when we pushed off the couch we may have felt disapproval for our desire to play independently. Or when we later returned from our time apart, our parents' anger at our departure may have caused them to be cold and distant when we tried to reengage.

Whatever the particulars, the result is that we might have determined that separation is bad. If you separate from the people who love you, they will be angry or hurt; then either you will feel guilty and have to take care of them, or they will be so angry that they won't love you anymore. A child who experiences this situation may then decide that separation is bad and togetherness is good.

Conversely, a child can grow up with a parent who is overstressed or overwhelmed and is relieved when the child goes off to play because he or she doesn't have to be emotionally present for the child. So when the child comes back from the hall, the parent isn't interested in connecting, and the child interprets connection and togetherness as a bad thing. If the parent is impatient and pushes the child away or scolds the child, the child will feel guilty about her need for togetherness and may feel a need to be separate.

This can function in reverse: If a child has a parent who always wants the child close, that child could grow up craving separateness. Because the child experienced togetherness as stifling, the natural desire for togetherness is seen as something to be suppressed and ignored because togetherness leads to being smothered. In the same way, the child that was pushed away and left alone might have become so starved for togetherness and so deprived of that kind of connection that she tries to bond deeply with others to make up for the deficit.

There are many ways to end up in a polarized position. Unfortunately, people usually pair up with their opposites. If you're comfortable with a great deal of separateness and not much togetherness, you'll very likely find yourself in relationships with individuals who are just the reverse because we are attracted to people who possess the strengths that we are trying to develop or aspects of ourselves that are lying dormant.

Figure 6.1

Sean doesn't understand that Teresa's need for separateness is different from his: "Don't you just love all this closeness?"

This attraction to opposites can create challenges in finding a comfortable balance of separateness and togetherness.

It is important that we are connected to other people, that we have a sense of belonging, unity, and being a part of something. It is also essential that we have a sense of autonomy, resilience, and self-reliance—a real sense of our ability to be in the world by ourselves so that we are not held hostage in our relationships. Let's look at how that dynamic functions in terms of distancing or pursuing others.

PURSUERS AND DISTANCERS

One of the biggest power struggles individuals go through is negotiating the amount of closeness and distance in their relationships. Each couple—friends, intimate partners, or coworkers—has its own intimacy distance. Just as people have personal physical space preferences, they also have personal intimacy space preferences. Imagine that your physical space preference is two feet. If someone stands or sits closer to you than two feet, you might feel uncomfortable and will likely try to move back to reestablish a more comfortable zone of two feet of physical space.

Much the same process occurs psychologically and emotionally. Let's say your intimacy comfort zone is a psychological five feet. In your case, this means that you like interacting with people to a certain extent, yet you really like your separateness. Anytime you manage to be with an individual whose intimacy distance matches yours, you will have a relatively even balance.

If, however, you are interacting with someone whose intimacy distance is three feet, that person will constantly move into your comfort zone another two feet, trying to close the distance to one that is more comfortable for them. That person may feel panicked and try to move closer because you are distant and remote. On the other hand, you will likely keep moving back, trying to reestablish your comfortable five feet of emotional distance.

The whole process of pursuing and distancing comes about because people want to be where they are comfortable. Unfortunately, those ways of behaving get some negative labels. People who tend to move closer often are labeled as clingy, smothering, and dependent. People who move away tend to be labeled cold, aloof, and unfeeling. In fact, personal distance is just a style preference, a difference in what allows a given individual to feel safe and comfortable.

What can you do about mismatched personal distances? It seems that usually a pursuer and a distancer hook up together. If you think about it, that pattern makes sense. Two people who are distancers and do nothing but distance each other are not going to have much of a relationship because there is not going to be much contact. Two people who are constantly pursuing each other are going to be with each other constantly and probably won't get anything else done. So even though it might feel frustrating in the moment, it is actually fortunate that we pair up that way.

If you are a pursuer, you probably wish the distancer in your life would move closer to you. That's what you identify as the sign of caring, because when you care about people, you want to move closer to them. What you need to do in order to change the dynamic from your end is to stop pursuing. For a week, try psychologically holding your ground; move neither away nor closer, and see how you feel. You might notice that you feel very anxious and panicky; you might not feel very emotionally connected, or you might feel adrift. Or you might notice that you feel just fine, that it was more of a habit than anything else. Whatever your reaction, hold your ground for a week, and keep track of how you feel. After the week is up, allow yourself a little breather by engaging as you normally do for a week; notice how you feel.

At the end of that second week, I want you to try something that is going to seem absurd. I want you to do behaviors that move you moderately away from the other person. You can do whatever fits in with your personality and style. I am not referring to doing anything dramatic like slamming doors or not talking to the other person for three days. I also don't mean that you should do anything in anger or anything unfeeling. I simply mean that if it is normally your habit to call your partner once during the day, don't do that.

Just pull back about one third on your seeking out and contacting behaviors. Do that for a week and notice how you feel. Sometimes you won't notice any change in the distancer's behavior for a while. But if you do this relatively consistently and without anger or hostility, after a while the distancer will start to move closer to you.

If you continue to hold your ground rather than move back toward the distancer when this occurs, that person will continue to pursue you. You might say, "Isn't this game playing when what I want to do is pursue the other person?" It isn't game playing because what you *really* want is a feeling of emotional closeness in the relationship. It's hard for a pursuer who is always pursuing to feel emotionally close because even when the partners are close, the pursuer feels that the distancer is on the verge of bolting at any moment. So if you can achieve the same amount of closeness with the distancer initiating, it's going to create a much deeper sense of safety.

Likewise for the distancer, if the pursuer can't seem to stop pursuing, one thing you can do to turn the dynamic around is to consistently, in small, manageable ways, start pursuing the pursuer. The pursuer may move closer initially. After a while though, the pursuer will probably start moving away. That will allow you to feel less trapped and smothered because suddenly you'll feel much more in control of the closeness. The more pursuing you do, the more distancing the pursuer in your life will gradually do. That person probably picked you because you knew how to create space and separateness in the relationship.

Once you reverse the pattern of your relationship by pursuing your partner, your partner will start creating part of the separateness in your relationship because every relationship strives for equilibrium. When this occurs, you may experience relief because suddenly you won't be seen as the bad, immature, selfish person who is always trying to be alone and apart. Both of you will start sharing the responsibility of creating space in the relationship, and both of you will benefit from the balancing of roles. The pursuer will feel wanted and attended to, and the distancer will stop feeling trapped, smothered, and cornered. You will both get to develop behaviors that you haven't developed as fully as the current behaviors that you habitually engage in, and that will strengthen both you and your partner.

NEGOTIATING RELATIONSHIP DIFFERENCES

Besides issues concerning togetherness and separateness, there are an endless number of potential relationship differences that two individuals must address. As a unique human being, you bring into the relationship your own preferences, opinions, styles, habits, and choices. The process of interweaving those personal elements in a healthy and workable manner with another person's equally unique set of preferences and beliefs can be incredibly challenging.

It is important to express your appreciation, acknowledgment, acceptance, and celebration of the other individual for the unique person he or she is while also doing the same for yourself. Your partner need not be a direct clone or carbon copy of you; not only is that not necessary, it would eventually become boring. A reasonable amount of difference makes a relationship more interesting and growth inducing because we tend to learn from people who are different from ourselves.

A crucial component in being able to learn from your partner's differences rather than be frustrated by them is the ability to negotiate or work through relationship differences when necessary. Imagine that I have a habit of leaving the cap off the toothpaste tube. Although I may view my habit as insignificant, someone else may experience it as incredibly irritating. The first step of negotiating is drawing on what you learned in Chapter Four about communicating your feelings clearly and being willing to compromise. Ideally my partner would communicate his discomfort with my habit and request that we generate some other options and negotiate a solution. We might solve this relationship difference by trying to brush our teeth at the same time and have my partner replace the cap each time. Or we might decide to buy toothpaste in a pump dispenser that has no cap.

Unfortunately, many relationship differences are much more significant than whether the cap is off the toothpaste. In those cases, such as an issue concerning monogamy and sexual fidelity, you and your partner need a framework to clearly resolve and concretely document your negotiations. One way to deal with negotiating significant relationship differences is to create a relationship agreement.

> Remember that a relationship in which it is impossible to negotiate and resolve differences is likely to be a continual source of pain.

A relationship agreement assumes that both people are reasonably healthy as individuals and are therefore able to bring a reasonably healthy self to the relationship. In addition, mutual trust, honesty, and integrity are present within each individual and are expressed toward each other. With these elements in place, a relationship negotiation agreement might take the form of the ambivalent partner agreeing to not act on sexual attraction to another person without first discussing the issue with the current partner. Another possible relationship agreement might be that if the ambivalent partner does become sexually intimate with someone else, he or she will engage in safe sex practices and inform the current partner of the sexual activity prior to resuming sexual activity with him or her. That way, the current partner isn't spared the emotional upheaval of the disruption of the relationship but is spared any health consequences from the other person's choice.

If you find yourself in a relationship where you cannot reasonably negotiate a relationship agreement and believe that the agreement will be agreed to, acted on, and honorably kept, then you are in a very dangerous place. Anyone who will not be honest and justifies lying to you puts you in a position of emotional and perhaps physical danger. You are simply not safe with someone who agrees to something but then violates the agreement and lies to you.

It is perfectly acceptable for people to decide that an earlier agreement no longer works or that they have outgrown the particulars of the agreement. However, it is absolutely lacking in integrity to agree to something and then not follow through on it while the other person proceeds as though the agreement is still in place. If someone can't keep an agreement, then you are in an environment of chaos where nothing can be acted upon or resolved. If you find yourself in such an environment, you may want to consider leaving the relationship.

It may be necessary to seek professional help in learning how to negotiate or to consider how well you are looking after your own well-being within the relationship. Remember that a relationship in which it is impossible to negotiate and resolve differences is likely to be a continual source of pain.

MEETING YOUR SHADOW SELF

What does it mean to meet your shadow self? It means looking at the part of yourself that you tend to keep hidden from others in the world. All of us have what I call a "daylight self"—the part of ourselves that we let others see and that we show to the world. It consists of the traits and aspects of our personalities that comprise our public self.

We also have a shadow self, which is the part of ourselves that, for whatever reason, we feel less comfortable with or less good about in some significant way. The shadow self contains what we consider to be our flaws and our embarrassments. Your shadow self is composed of all the aspects of yourself that you feel discomfort or shame about possessing. It consists of all the things about yourself that you would rather not look at or acknowledge. All of the characteristics about yourself that you have decided are unacceptable or that you must not show to others are contained in your shadow self.

In addition, your shadow self contains aspects of yourself that you may not have conscious awareness of. In fact, you may believe that exactly the opposite is true about yourself. Suppose a woman sees her-

Figure 6.2

Ted meets his shadow self.

self as utterly courageous and fearless, but in reality she is terrified of the part of herself that is appropriately fearful. She hides her fearful side from others (and perhaps herself) within her shadow self. She probably reacts to fearfulness in others with judgment and disapproval because it is virtually impossible to accept in others what you have dis-owned in yourself.

Exactly that dynamic of reacting to others with extreme judgment and disapproval can assist you in identifying what is contained in your shadow self. Anytime you notice yourself harshly evaluating another person, chances are that they express a piece of your shadow self. Rather than judge, you can instead ask yourself, "What is this person doing or saying that expresses some aspect of myself that I feel is unacceptable and therefore must make unacceptable in this person?"

By answering this question, you not only gain insight into the nature and contents of your shadow self, but you also move from a place of judging to a position of noticing. Instead of judging, "He shouldn't be so self-centered," you instead notice, "I am unaccepting of his self-focus because I feel that if I did that no one would love me, so therefore it and he must be bad."

In the process of gaining and articulating awareness, you shift your focus from judging and attempting to change the other person to notic-ing what part of yourself you have disowned. Once you are aware of what you have disowned, you can ask yourself, "What portion of what I have disowned would I like to reclaim for myself?" This process is the first step toward accepting and valuing all of yourself—including the parts of yourself that you like the least. It is also a crucial step toward increasing your self-esteem. It is difficult to have a solid sense of self-esteem when you feel that much of yourself must be hidden from others. By choosing to assimilate and accept part of each disowned piece of the shadow self, you are in effect saying that all aspects of yourself are worth having and loving.

Self-acceptance becomes especially crucial once you choose to be in a relationship. If you enter a relationship unaware of your shadow self, you may unconsciously choose a partner who openly expresses aspects of your shadow self. Because you are not aware of or do not accept the qualities contained in your shadow self, you may find yourself harshly criticizing your partner for behaviors or qualities that your partner is expressing in appropriate ways and proportions. And lack of self-awareness is one of the major ways we unwittingly damage one another in relationships, because when we lack accurate self-knowledge we are not able to provide those we love with clear information regarding who we truly are, what we are actually capable of, and what they can expect from us. And when we disown our shadow aspects, we further confuse our loved ones by taking the stance that something true about us isn't in fact true, and instead try to convince them that this unacceptable trait is actually true about them.

Often much of what seems unworkable in relationships is actually the projection of disowned shadow-self material on the other partner.

In addition, because of your inability to accept those same qualities or behaviors in yourself, you may exaggerate the extent to which your partner expresses your shadow-self qualities. This process can result in your managing to fully disown an aspect of yourself, such as anger, and instead projecting all of your disowned anger on your partner. Then you can judge your partner as overly angry while you continue to view yourself as a calm person who, for some strange reason, keeps attracting angry partners.

Often much of what seems unworkable in relationships is actually the projection of disowned shadow-self material on the other partner. One way to help bring the relationship back in balance is to ask yourself, "What does my partner overexpress in this relationship that I perhaps underexpress?" Your answer will often raise your awareness of your shadow-self aspects.

There are obvious exceptions to this dynamic. If your partner is emotionally abusive, violent, or homicidal, that in no way implies that you have those aspects hidden away in your shadow self or that you need to increase your expression of those traits. What I am referring to are relationship issues—power, anger, responsibility, motivation, depression, expression of emotions—that tend to be overexpressed by one partner and underexpressed by another.

A good first step in beginning to share the expression of these shadow aspects is to ask yourself, "Am I willing to reclaim a piece of what it seems my partner is overdoing?" Assuming your answer is yes, your next step is to identify when you legitimately could express some of what your partner is overdoing. If your partner overdoes anger, pay close attention to when *you* begin to feel anger and when you shut those feelings off. Your next step is to say, "I'm feeling angry," and allow yourself to feel any emotions that arise from it.

Gradually, as you begin to reclaim your disowned anger, your partner will become less angry because you are taking responsibility for your share of the expression of that emotion. In addition to increased self-esteem, one of the greatest benefits of reclaiming your disowned shadow self is that it helps shift your relationship from one of blame and judgment to a relationship of acceptance and shared responsibility. Your relationship will feel friendlier and more supportive as you and your partner realize that you both share ownership of the various emotions contained within the relationship.

Here are some exercises that will help you begin to personalize the information presented in this chapter. Begin by writing yourself a prescription for self-awareness.

Rx FOR SELF-AWARENESS

1. A healthy relationship for me means that

   _____

   _____

2. When someone wants separateness or space, I

   _____

   _____

3. When someone wants lots of togetherness, I

   _____

   _____

4. What I most like from a partner is

   _____

   _____

5. What I least like from a partner is

   _____

   _____

6. What makes a relationship unhealthy for me is

   _____

   _____

7. One way that I pursue others is

   _____

   _____

8. One way that I distance myself from others is

   _____

   _____

9. The thing I'd most like to negotiate with a partner is

   _____

   _____

10. A part of my shadow self that I'd most like to accept is

-----

11. If I could learn only one new thing about relationships, I'd like to learn

-----

FOR YOUR JOURNAL . . .

1. What did you learn about yourself from this chapter?
2. How does that change things for you or help you make sense of your life?
3. What else do you want to know about yourself?

RECOMMENDED READINGS

Bly, Robert. 1992. *A Little Book on the Human Shadow.* New York: HarperCollins.

Explores the shadow side of human personality and the need to examine, confront, and reclaim this part of the self.

DeAngelis, Barbara. 1993. *Are You the One for Me?* New York: Bantam Doubleday Dell.

Discusses how to evaluate the appropriateness of a potential partner and how to make healthy, thoughtful choices to create fulfilling relationships.

Goldschneider, Gary and Effers, Joost. 1997. *The Secret Language of Relationships: Your Complete Personality Guide to Any Relationship with Anyone.* Penguin Studio.

Looks at the hows and whys of chemistry in relationships and explores relationships dynamics.

Gray, John. 1992. *Men Are From Mars, Women Are From Venus.* New York: HarperCollins.

Uncovers fundamental differences in the way women and men communicate, feel, and behave, and suggests how to cope effectively with these differences.

Hendrix, Harville. 1992. *Getting the Love You Want.* New York: Harper and Row.

Assists in creating more support, understanding, and satisfying resolutions of conflicts in your relationship through a step-by-step ten-week set of exercises.

Peabody, Susan. 1996. *Addiction to Love: Overcoming Obsession and Dependency in Relationships.* Berkeley, CA: Ten Speed Press.

Explains how dependency is not related to romantic love and provides useful steps to help the reader break out of addictive relationships.

Tannen, Deborah. 1991. *You Just Don't Understand.* New York: William Morrow.

Describes with supporting theory and examples the reasons underlying the differences in the way men and women communicate and encourages understanding and acceptance of these differences.

A NEW SENSE
OF DIRECTION

NEEDS, WANTS, AND VALUES

What do you absolutely need to survive? Food, water, clothing, medical care when ill or injured—anything else? All of us have our own internal list of what we feel we need in order to run our lives smoothly. How about winning the lottery for starters? Perhaps this falls into a category other than need, but we'll get to that later in this chapter. For now, start by making a list of the things you need to have in your life. Don't concern yourself with whether something you list is a legitimate need or whether someone would disapprove of what's on your list. Do your best to shut out those external critical voices as you make your list.

Q

A

Your list of needs

1. _____   9. _____
2. _____   10. _____
3. _____   11. _____
4. _____   12. _____
5. _____   13. _____
6. _____   14. _____
7. _____   15. _____
8. _____

Physical _____   Emotional _____   Mental _____   Spiritual _____

Don't be concerned if you couldn't generate 15 needs or if you have a longer list. There is no right or wrong way to do this exercise.

Now, read through your list. Circle the items you listed that are absolutely necessary for your physical survival. Look at the uncircled items on your list. What aspects of your well-being do those items focus on? Do they meet emotional, mental, spiritual, or nonsurvival physical needs?

Count up the needs in each of the four categories. Do your needs cluster in any one area? Let's look at Tracey's need list as an example:

Tracey's List of Needs

1. food	P
2. water	P
3. shelter	P
4. safety of my children	P
5. heat (during the winter)	P
6. medical care	P
7. transportation	P
8. air to breathe	P
9. a loving relationship	E
10. a peaceful environment	E
11. challenging job	M
12. alone time	E
13. connection to my higher power	S
14. good support network	E
15. plenty of books to read	M

Physical __8__   Emotional __4__   Mental __2__   Spiritual __1__

Notice that Tracey put a P, E, M, or S by each item on her list so she could remember if she counted each item as a physical, emotional, mental, or spiritual need. She then counted the needs and entered the totals in the spaces provided. In Tracey's case, most needs fell into the physical category.

Now look back at your need list. Look again at the circled items. Are these things you absolutely require in order to survive, or are they instead very important preferences that would be painful to be without?

NEEDS VS. WANTS

At this point, I'd like you to consider that any item not directly connected with basic physical survival is a want or desire rather than an actual need. You might be thinking, what's the big deal about saying want instead of need? On one level, you're absolutely right—it's just a matter of substituting one word for another. But our use of language affects us on more than just a surface level. Language shapes how we think about ourselves and the world, which in turn shapes our beliefs; and our beliefs shape our feelings about ourselves, others, and the world around us. Let's look at how this works by returning to Tracey's want list. Tracey has listed a loving relationship as one of her needs. Try saying out loud, "I *need* a loving relationship." Now say, "I *want* a loving relationship." Does saying one sentence make you feel more desperate or anxious? Does another sentence make you feel more powerful, more in control of yourself?

For most people, saying "I need" brings up feelings of desperation, panic, clutchiness, powerlessness, and insecurity. When you hear the word "needy," what words come to mind? My guess is that many of the same words that come up when you say "I need" also fit your definition of needy. Avoiding unpleasant feelings of neediness is why it's important to try to use the word "need" only to describe a genuine need.

Another reason to work on separating your needs and wants is that the word "want" conveys a far greater sense of power than does the word "need." Want implies a personal choice to emphasize or value a specific person, thing, or experience. Want is about choosing to desire something, whereas need is about having to depend on or manipulate someone into giving you something that you feel you must have. If you want something, you can try to create a way to fill that want—you can take the responsibility for filling that want. You have the power to work toward giving yourself what you desire.

But what if you were taught that it is selfish or wrong to want things? What if you feel too visible or vulnerable declaring your wants? Part of the reason many of us have trouble acknowledging or expressing our wants is that we were taught that it was okay to need things that were undeniably necessary, but simply wanting something meant that we were selfish, spoiled, never satisfied, weak, or just plain bad. If you were taught this, then how do you overcome these feelings?

One of the best ways I know to reframe wanting as a positive, healthy, appropriate characteristic is to think of a cat or dog you have known. One of the most wonderful things about animals is their ability to simply want what they want in the moment without judging that wanting. My cat, Spike, is very fond of being scratched under the chin; when she wants to be scratched, she hops up on my desk and rubs her head against my hand. She doesn't wonder if it's reasonable to want what she wants, or if she has a right to want it, or if she's worth it—she simply asks for what she wants.

We could learn a good deal from such straightforward behavior. If we could learn to simply ask for what we want, our lives would be much simpler and perhaps much more satisfying. Asking for what we want won't necessarily get us what we want; we may feel disappointed sometimes. But if we take responsibility for asking, we stand a better chance of getting some of what we want from others. And if we don't get what we want from others, we can decide whether to create those things for ourselves.

First you need to know what your wants are. Take a moment to list any wants that occur to you.

Q   *Your list of wants*

1. _____	9. _____
2. _____	10. _____
3. _____	11. _____
4. _____	12. _____
A	5. _____	13. _____
6. _____	14. _____
7. _____	15. _____
8. _____	

Once you've created a wants list, a clear knowledge of your values can make the decision-making process a matter of checking how a particular want matches up with your values. Ready to give it a try? Great—let's take a look at values.

VALUES

Clarity about your most important values and beliefs can help make navigating life transitions a less confusing process. Let's say Robin's marriage is ending, and Robin is faced with a choice between living alone and sharing an apartment with a friend. If Robin is feeling any mixture of shock, pain, grief, numbness, and disbelief, she may feel unable to decide what to eat for dinner, much less where to live. However, if Robin could pull out a handy, personalized value summary and life philosophy (as you'll be able to do once you've completed this chapter), she could compare the options against her most important values. If one of Robin's most significant values is solitude, she can use that piece of knowledge to help shape the final decision.

One of the most difficult aspects of a transition is the sense of beginning to doubt everything you thought you knew. That's why I suggested in the introduction that you respond in writing to the queries and exercises in this book, so that you can refer to these responses during future transitions. One of the most important components of your written record is going to be the section containing your values and life philosophy, for they will guide your way through each transition.

One of the most difficult aspects of a transition is the sense of beginning to doubt everything you thought you knew.

So what exactly are values? Before we discuss what values are and go through some value awareness exercises, I want you to make a list of what you think your values are right now at this point in your life. Don't worry if you're not sure what a value is; just make your best guess. Later you'll compare this list to your final values list. So just give it your best attempt.

Your list of values

1. _____   9. _____
2. _____   10. _____
3. _____   11. _____
4. _____   12. _____
5. _____   13. _____
6. _____   14. _____
7. _____   15. _____
8. _____

Now put this list aside while we explore values. What exactly are values? Values are:

* learned from parents, friends, and significant role models
* evolving, changing aspects of your personality

- based on individual, personal preferences and priorities
- crucial determining factors in making good decisions
- revealed in your choices, comments, and actions

Let's look at these points one at a time.

Values Are Learned

As we grow and develop as children, we are bound to be affected by the values of our families and significant others. Often what we think are values that we've freely chosen as adults are actually values that were passed on to us from our families. We often accepted and incorporated those values as our own without ever considering whether they accurately reflected our thoughts and feelings. There is nothing wrong with having learned and adopted values in this way, but it's important to examine how we came to call them our own. Let's take a look at how this occurred.

Q

Make a list of ten things that family members told you were important:

1. _____   6. _____
2. _____   7. _____
3. _____   8. _____
A
4. _____   9. _____
5. _____   10. _____

Q

1. Does your list contain primarily positive or negative things?

   _____

2. Circle the things you still agree with. Pick one thing you don't agree with and explain why.

A
   _____

   _____

3. What is difficult about disagreeing with your family's values?

   _____

   _____

4. How does disagreeing make your life harder?

   _____

   _____

5. Are there any values you would like to unlearn?

_____

_____

_____

6. Are there any values you'd like to add to your current set of values?

_____

_____

_____

Values Evolve

Most of us can think back to our childhood and remember values that seemed crucial to our well-being at the time but that no longer hold the same importance or worth to us now. As a teenager I wanted to be just like my friends in the clothes I wore and what I did socially on the weekends. Back then, standing out as different or unique in any way felt intolerable. Now as an adult I value the uniqueness and individuality of others far more than someone's ability to blend in. Part of the reason our values change is that as we take in and process new information and experiences, we learn, grow, and change. As a result, what we deem important shifts and changes.

> Part of the reason our values change is that as we take in and process new information and experiences, we learn, grow, and change.

Values Are Based on Individual Preferences and Priorities

Each term I like to have students in my Life Transitions class do the "stranded studio apartment" exercise.

 Imagine that you are in your favorite outdoor environment. It can be in the mountains, in the desert, by a lake, or by the ocean. Assume that you've been stranded in this environment with no way out and that there is no way for civilization to reach you. You might be on a remote island or near the top of an unscalable mountain peak. Although you're stranded, you discover you have access to an ample-sized studio apartment equipped with basic supplies for your comfort such as indoor plumbing, heat, hot and cold water, furniture, bedding, cookware, clothing, food, a refrigerator, a stove, a washer, a dryer, and toiletries. Now imagine that you get to add six things or people of your choosing to this environment. What six things or people would you choose? You may count all of your children as one choice, but any other people count as one choice each.

Your list of choices

1. _____   4. _____

2. _____   5. _____

3. _____   6. _____

Take a look at your choices. Can you pick out the values embedded in each choice? Let's look at my list as an example:

1. my cat   4. TV with satellite dish

2. my partner   5. phone with unlimited long
                                  distance

3. lots of books   6. exercise equipment

When I try to identify the values on my list or on one of my students' lists, I look for basic themes. One good way to find those themes is to ask the person to explain why each item is on the list. My cat and my partner are on my list for the same reason: because I enjoy and value the connection, companionship, and relationships that I have with each of them. I included a phone for a similar reason: I would want to maintain my relationships with a number of people even though we were geographically separated. Books are on my list because I love to learn new things, and reading is one of my favorite ways to learn. I have a television on my list because some of my favorite forms of entertainment are old movies, stand-up comics, and music. Exercise equipment is on my list because working out is crucial to my sense of wellness and well-being. The basic themes that I can extract from my list are:

* connection and companionship
* learning
* entertainment
* wellness

I can translate those basic themes into a partial list of my values. I value:

* connected relationships with significant others
* knowledge and the learning process
* lightheartedness, fun, and relaxation
* physical well-being and a general sense of wellness

Feel ready to give it a try with your list? Good. Feel free to work with classmates or friends to help each other identify themes and values. Don't worry if your list doesn't seem to be a complete representation of your values—it's not supposed to be at this point. Just do this piece for now, and you'll add more to it as we continue.

Values Are Crucial to Good Decision Making

First of all, what constitutes good decision making? Good decision making means making decisions that align with who you are as an individual and that support your goals and life purpose. A wonderful decision for you could be horrendous when applied to someone else's life.

Values serve as a kind of internal decision compass, helping us steer our way through confusing or conflicting situations. If I place a high value on fidelity and loyalty, then when a gorgeous stranger asks me out, the decision I need to make is clear (although I may experience a pang or two). However, if my values of fidelity and loyalty compete with equally strong values of excitement and adventure, I may have to choose one set of values over another. Which set of values I decide is most important will largely determine whether I accept the date.

Values serve as a kind of internal decision compass, helping us steer our way through confusing or conflicting situations.

At this point in my class someone usually says, "Wait a minute. Some values are simply wrong, and no matter how you justify them, it still doesn't make them right." I agree. You'll never hear me argue that abusing children or adults is an acceptable value. However, some values may seem absolutely "wrong" to you and yet utterly "right" to someone else.

You get to have your values no matter what anyone else thinks or wants. There may be religious groups, political groups, family, friends, or coworkers who disagree with your values. Fine—this isn't about achieving group consensus, it's about staying true to your values regardless of whether others approve. It's about using your values as a stable foundation on which to build your choices and life direction. Remember that values can change as you mature. With new information, insights, and experiences, your values may gradually shift, radically change, or be reaffirmed.

Values are also culturally based. Traits valued in the Western world are not universally experienced or valued in other cultures. I encourage you to expose yourself to other cultural perspectives as a way to expand your awareness of other values and belief systems that you may not have considered.

Values Are Revealed in Your Choices, Comments, and Actions

Remember the Brag Sheet Exercise from Chapter Five? Turn back to your responses for that exercise and look at what you wrote. Can you determine the values woven into your answers? Add those values to your value list.

Do the same thing for your responses to the questions about your shadow self at the end of Chapter Six. Notice what values emerge when you look through these answers; if there are any new values that you don't already have on your list, add them.

Here's another way to help you uncover your values. What do you do with free time? Whether you structure your life so that you never have any, spend it all with family, or spend it alone, each choice suggests a different value.

In addition, there may be things you yearn to do that internally feel like values but that you're not living out yet in your life. Think about what these values are, add them to your list, and circle them as a reminder to commit yourself to acting on those values when possible.

Whatever your values are, be real about what they are. Start by being truthful with yourself, truthful with others, and truthful with the world. You may lose some opportunities and relationships through your realness, but the consequences of consistently pretending your values are different from what they truly are causes you to lose an honest sense of yourself. While there may be certain circumstances where it is not wise to share your full array of values, there are many other situations in which this is both possible and prudent.

One other exercise may assist you in discerning additional values. Your home has caught fire. All living creatures are safely outside. What are the first three things you would save? Identify the values involved and add them to your list.

Special Note to Female Readers

Each term that I teach Life Transitions, I have the students take a value inventory survey. After everyone has completed it, I ask each person to give me the two most important values and the two least important values from the rating sheets. The lowest values for women are almost always power and recognition. When I ask the class why these values are rated so low, the women describe negative connotations of those words.

When women think of recognition, they usually think of a woman who is obnoxiously yammering on and on about how terrific she is, exaggerating her abilities and contributions embarrassingly out of proportion, and expecting lots of attention from others. Power brings to mind even more negative images. Power is seen as abuse of power, as control and domination over those less strong. No wonder most women rate these values as undesirable and unimportant.

I'd like you to reconsider recognition as an appropriate appreciation and celebration of your strengths and abilities. Think about a five-year-old girl racing home from kindergarten with a paper full of newly written ABCs to ecstatically share her accomplishment. She hasn't yet been trained to pretend her accomplishment is no big deal, to wait until someone notices it, or to worry that someone will think she has a big head if she shows how proud she is. She simply is experiencing pleasure in her achievement and wants to share that with others. We could learn a lot from her healthy perspective.

Think about the difference between power *over* versus power *to be able to.* The women in my class were rejecting power over others—domineering, controlling, abusive power. Power to be able to means power to change and control your day-to-day life and to shape your future. Who doesn't want that kind of power?

DEVELOPING A POSITIVE ATTITUDE TOWARD CHANGE

For both men and women, an important step in claiming power is using that power to create and maintain a positive attitude toward change. Being able to do that will dramatically stabilize the ups and downs and greatly improve the quality of your life.

Since so much of your life is going to be spent in the midst of change or significant life transition, you might as well enjoy as much of it as possible.

What if you hate change? What if you're the kind of person who gets hives just moving the furniture around the living room? Am I really saying that somebody like you has to get comfortable with change rather than just gritting your teeth and surviving it? Yes, that's exactly what I'm saying. Since so much of your life is going to be spent in the midst of change or significant life transition, you might as well enjoy as much of it as possible.

So how do you do that? A crucial step in developing a positive attitude toward change is to learn how to make the change or changes you're facing uniquely yours. My cat Spike throws a fit whenever I rearrange the furniture; she does her best with glares and loud scratching to get me to undo the change. When that fails, she marks each piece of moved furniture by rubbing the side of her head against the furniture. While I'm not suggesting that you deal with changes and transitions in exactly the same way, it is essential to claim the change as your own.

So many people feel change is something that just happens to them, something that strikes out of nowhere and disrupts their lives. They fail to see change as a part of their lives and instead look at it as an outside

Figure 7.1

Staying positive keeps Maria afloat during tough transitions.

force that louses things up just as they're going really well. As long as you feel that change is an outside force that needs to be minimized, you are at risk of continually feeling (and perhaps behaving) like someone perpetually on the verge of being victimized.

Have you ever been around someone who says, "This is too good to be true; there's no way it's ever going to last"? Did you notice that no matter how much others urge him to just enjoy how well things are going, he resists doing that because he'll "only feel worse when it ends"? Well, things end—both good experiences and painful experiences. If you strive to avoid the pain of change and the endings that accompany change, you'll expend a tremendous amount of energy. In addition, avoiding change creates an atmosphere of dread and impending gloom that tends to overshadow any joy and pleasure in your life.

Since change is going to happen anyway, you might as well enjoy it. Cultivating a sense of humor is one of the best ways I know to build and maintain a positive attitude toward change. One of my favorite ways to cope with change is to picture change shuffling up to my front door. I could respond by bolting the door, locking the windows, and closing the blinds, but instead I throw the front door open, sit down on the couch, pat the seat cushion, and yell, "Come on down, you're the next contes-

Figure 7.2

Carl hears his life changes knocking and invites them in.

tant in Cara's changing existence!" Truly silly, but why not be the emcee of your life? Even if you can't control change, you do have control over your attitude and how you cope with change.

A good friend of mine believes that we should have theme music playing in the background of our lives just as people do in the movies. He hums the theme from *Jaws* when facing an especially challenging transition. Think about what makes you laugh and try to incorporate an aspect of that into your changes and life transitions.

COMPOSING YOUR LIFE PHILOSOPHY

Another important component in developing and maintaining a positive attitude toward change is having a clear and concise image of who you are, what you value, and how you want to relate to the world. By creating a life philosophy that reminds you of both your hopes and your purpose, it is easier to keep a positive frame of mind while going through a life transition. A life philosophy serves not only as a statement of who you are and how you want to live your life, but also as a substantial stabilizing force in the midst of transition. While parts of it may shift as you move through your transitions, much of it will remain constant. Your life philosophy can help you remain centered and remind you of how much you know and how much clarity you have.

One of the most useful functions of a life philosophy is its ability to serve as a link between your values and your life goals. A life philosophy contains your core values and beliefs, and reminds you of what your larger vision is as you make choices and decisions designed to help you reach your life goals. Your life philosophy is your individual tapestry woven out of your hopes and beliefs—your hope of where you might be, hope of what this transition will hold for you, the belief in yourself, your abilities, your connections with others, your beliefs regarding what your life is about. It is the things you find solace and inspiration in as you face the unknown, trusting in all that you still know, even as you take the leap into the next unknown phase of your life.

It may seem ironic that the payoff for scaling all the rock barriers that we've previously discussed is a mind-boggling moment of truth on the top of the cliff, as you face the need to leap into the next unfolding facet of your life. It is at that moment—at the juncture between your life prior to this current transition and your future, unknowable life—that your life philosophy proves invaluable. Having a clear sense of who you are, what you care about, what you deeply value written down on paper gives you both a literal and symbolic way to hold onto and give attention to the core elements of who you are during a time when nearly everything else in your life may be shifting and changing.

Rather than getting caught up in the endless self-doubt that most people experience in the midst of transition, by writing a life philosophy you can create enduring clarity regarding where you draw meaning. You can create a vision of what matters most to you, your reasons why you are not only going to sustain yourself through this transition, but why you are on the planet, what it is that you are here to contribute, why you will decide to care at all about contending with the challenges and issues that each new transition brings. Your life philosophy consists of threads of your past, moments when you've reconsidered your views and self-concept, values and beliefs that have sustained you through difficult times, and experiences that have challenged you to grow and shaped your vision of the world. Once completed, your life philosophy can remind you of your history, to hold a sense of hope and wonder in the world, to encompass what you value and cherish most, and to reflect the beauty and enduring nature of your life.

All of that wonderful promotion aside, this is the exercise that gets the loudest groans, sighs, whimpers, and "you've got to be kidding" comments from my students. I promise that this will be easier than it seems at first glance. I'm going to provide seven questions for you to respond to, and if you write out your responses as though you were just telling a good friend, you'll move through this easily. Talk into a tape recorder first if that makes it more comfortable for you. Just let the answers to one question flow into the next.

Don't worry about spelling or punctuation—the important thing is to communicate what is important to you. You may want to pull out your values list and other exercises you've done so that you can refer to them as you respond to each question. I always tell students to use at least one paragraph to respond to each question. (Feel free to write more if you'd like.) Using that guideline will force you to construct a response, even if you'd like to avoid answering a certain question. Ready?

Q   Questions to respond to in writing your life philosophy:

1. Who am I and who am I becoming?

A   _____

_____

_____

_____

_____

_____

2. What are my guiding beliefs and values?

_____

_____

_____

_____

_____

_____

3. What motivates and inspires me?

_____

_____

_____

_____

_____

_____

4. What do I need to do to take responsibility for my life?

_____

_____

_____

_____

_____

5. What is my life purpose—what am I here to contribute?

_____

_____

_____

_____

_____

6. What kind of world do I want to live in?

_____

_____

_____

_____

_____

7. What will I do to leave the world a better place?

_____

_____

_____

_____

_____

When you're done writing this, read it aloud, change things, add things, and do your best to make it thoroughly reflect all that you know about yourself. Then I want you to print it, frame it, and put it somewhere you'll see it every day. You can temporarily take it down if you have company and don't want to share it with them. Keeping your life philosophy in front of you will help you survive all those mornings that you drag yourself out of bed and wonder if there's really a point to what you're doing and if you even know what you're doing (everyone has those days). You know what you're doing, and you know why it's important to you. You may not yet know how to get to where you're headed because you've never attempted that journey before. Just remember, you already know the most important things—yourself, your values, and your life philosophy—and you'll figure out the details as you move in your chosen direction. You just completed the toughest part of this process. Congratulations!

Here are some exercises that will help you begin to personalize the information presented in this chapter. Begin by writing a prescription for self-awareness.

R̪ FOR SELF-AWARENESS

1. What I most want from life is

    _____

    _____

    _____

2. Something I want that no one else knows is

    _____

    _____

3. Some of my most important values are

    _____

    _____

4. When I don't live in alignment with my values I feel

    _____

    _____

5. What I most value about change is

    _____

    _____

6. What I find most difficult about change is

_____

_____

7. How I use my sense of humor to cope with change is

_____

_____

8. My hopes about this transition are

_____

_____

9. Things I find solace and inspiration in are

_____

_____

10. My abilities that I value and trust are

_____

_____

11. One belief involved in my positive attitude is

_____

_____

FOR YOUR JOURNAL . . .

1. What did you learn about yourself from this chapter?
2. How does that change things for you or help you make sense of your life?
3. What else do you want to know about yourself?

RECOMMENDED READINGS

Arrien, Angeles. 1993. *The Four-Fold Way.* New York: HarperCollins.
Explores the four archetypes present in many cultural traditions and demonstrates how appropriate development and expression of all four archetypes can help individuals heal themselves and society.

Capen, Richard. 1996. *Finish Strong: Living the Values that Take You the Distance.* New York: Harper.

Shows how to develop strong personal values and how they can be nurtured.

Carter, Steven and Sokol, Julia. 1995. *He's Scared, She's Scared.* New York: Delacorte Press.

Explains the sources and types of commitment fears and conflicts, and offers ways to overcome them.

Matthews, Andrew. 1990. *Being Happy!* Los Angeles: Price Stern Sloan.

A light-hearted, easy-to-read book that focuses on increasing self-awareness, self-confidence, self-forgiveness, and goal-achievement.

Peck, M. Scott. 1998. *The Road Less Traveled.* New York: Simon and Schuster.

Encourages the reader to face reality, confront personal problems and limitations, and seek appropriate resolutions.

Seligman, Martin. 1998. *Learned Optimism.* New York: Simon and Schuster.

Offers tests to assess your current level of pessimism or optimism and how it influences your life. Assists in helping you learn to be more optimistic.

Taulbert, Clifton. 1997. *Eight Habits of the Heart: The Timeless Values that Build Strong Commitments.* Viking Press.

Explores eight different values, including a nurturing attitude, dependability, friendship, brotherhood, courage, and hope, and demonstrates how engaging in these values can increase well-being.

SETTING YOUR COMPASS

GOAL AND OBJECTIVE SETTING

Goals are the end points we set for ourselves—the finish lines that we set in different areas of our lives. If you think of a goal as the destination of a road trip—say you want to travel to a town 100 miles away—that town 100 miles away is your goal. It's the place you want to end up. It's important to use your values, goals, and objectives rather than someone else's. Otherwise, you'll end up where they wanted to go rather than where you wanted to go.

Objectives are the small rest stops, gas stations, and towns you pass along the way that help you reach your end point. An objective is a minigoal that helps you take a step to reach your goal. Merely setting a goal and then expecting to achieve it rarely works for most people because most of us need to have big goals broken down into small, manageable pieces. Objectives are bite-sized chunks of your larger goal. Think of objectives as your "to do" list for your goals.

You can also think of goals and objectives in relation to the cliff-diving transitions model. Your goal is to successfully complete your dive into the next transition. Your objectives are each handhold you use to help yourself climb over the rocks and reach your goal.

In addition, goals are like having a compass. You start in a certain direction with your goal. Even if you change your mind and later set an entirely new goal, the act of starting off in a certain direction causes you to commit to heading somewhere, to commit to action.

Figure 8.1

Follow your own path and trust your vision of where you want to go.

When people manage to create aspects of their lives that they're happy with, they usually have done so by setting goals. Their original goals and the goals that they achieve may not be remotely related. But once they have moved out in the world, they are in and around opportunities and are able to actively watch and experience life situations with an eye for how things can help them achieve their goals.

When people manage to create aspects of their lives that they're happy with, they usually have done so by setting goals.

Goals can be created for any aspect of your life: personal, emotional, relationship, health, career, spiritual, or financial. You can make a goal in relation to anything by deciding what you want next for yourself and committing yourself to action. Setting goals makes the difference between taking what life offers you and creating what you want for yourself.

Setting goals and acting on them are often very difficult, even when you know that doing so will benefit you. You may find it hard to set goals because as a child your home environment was so chaotic and disrupted that there was no opportunity to focus on anything but dealing with the latest crisis. You were unable to focus on yourself, on your growth, and on determining what you wanted.

Or perhaps you knew what you wanted but grew up in a family where no one set goals, where people just let life happen to them; and you had no role models for how someone can set a goal, act on it, and achieve it. Or you may have come from a family that penalized you for setting goals and achieving them, especially if you surpassed other family members.

So, let's practice articulating goals and developing objectives that allow you to move closer to your goals. First, remember that a goal is simply the result or outcome you'd like to create or achieve for yourself in a certain area of your life. Second, objectives are merely the steps, behaviors, or tasks that you need to do in order to reach your goal. The more specific, measurable, and positive your goal is, the better your chances of reaching it. Thus, "I don't want to do unhealthy things anymore" is not a clear goal as it is not specific, measurable, or positive—and it's impossible to know if and when you've achieved it. On the other hand, "I will lower my cholesterol reading by 10 points" gives you a clear sense of the envisioned goal and a way to judge whether you've successfully achieved it.

In a similar fashion, it is most productive to set your goal-related objectives as small, incremental steps—the smaller the better. So, "have some healthy food in the house" isn't very useful as an objective, but "go to the store and purchase three different kinds of fresh fruit" is because it's clear and easy to accomplish. And when objectives are easy to accomplish, they serve to both move you steadily toward your goal and keep your enthusiasm and motivation high.

Goals and objectives are two of the main components in constructing an action plan. There are many ways to construct an action plan and many forms an action plan can take. The action plan format that I'll be sharing with you is the one that my students and I have found most useful. As I guide you through this process, follow along by writing your responses in the blank action plan below.

Creating an Action Plan

The first step in creating an action plan is to identify a goal on which you want to take action. Remember to make your goal specific, measurable, and positive. Second, list the first five objectives you would like to tackle to move you closer to your goal. Again, remember to make your objectives small, achievable steps.

Next, consider your time frame for both achieving your goal and completing your objectives. Most goals will require many more than just five objectives to achieve them, but trying to make an exhaustive list of all of the steps to achieve your goal usually is too overwhelming and discouraging for most people, so I suggest that you tackle the objectives in chunks of five until you reach your goal. Simply update the objectives section of your action plan each time you are on the verge of completing that set of objectives.

Once you've established your time frame, make a list of your three largest potential obstacles that you might encounter as you strive towards your goal. Next, consider what your approach would be if you did encounter that obstacle—how would you handle it? The next step in creating your action plan is to contemplate what your three largest potential gains might be once you've successfully achieved your goal. The final step in creating your action plan is to write an affirmation for achieving your goal. Your affirmation should take the form discussed in Chapter Five, and it should be a positive expression related to achieving your goal.

Below is an action plan example, with a blank action plan following the example plan. I encourage you to experiment with writing action plans for any area of your life in which you are facing change. In addition, share your goals with others, write them down rather than just thinking them, and post your goals somewhere visible. By doing this, you convey to yourself and others that you are taking your goals seriously, and as difficult as the goal-setting process can be, you deepen and cement your commitment to the process and to yourself by doing this.

DECISION MAKING AND RISK TAKING

Another thing that makes goals difficult is the issue of decision making and risk taking. Decision making is something most people struggle with. Decision making feels risky for most people because of the fear of choosing the wrong thing. The toughest thing about decision making is that most choices cause you to give up and lose things. Remember the discussion in Chapter Three about the fact that every time we choose something, we also lose something? The same notion applies to decision making. Making one decision often immediately eliminates the option of making other decisions.

Action Plan Example

GOAL:	TIME FRAME:
Lower my cholesterol reading by 10 points	3 months

OBJECTIVES:

1.	eat three servings of fresh fruit daily	this week
2.	walk 20 minutes each day	this week
3.	eat 3 eggs or less per week	this week
4.	substitute olive oil for butter in two meals	this week
5.	buy a low-fat cookbook; try 12 new recipes	by 3 weeks from today

THREE OBSTACLES:	COPING STRATEGY:
1. lack of time	get up earlier to fit walking in
2. bad weather for walking	get rain gear or treadmill
3. tasteless low-fat cooking	ask others for their best recipes

THREE GAINS:

1. have a healthier heart
2. feel physically better and have more energy
3. set good role model for the kids

POSITIVE AFFIRMATION: I create physical health by my wise choices each day.

Action Plan Worksheet

GOAL: TIME FRAME:

OBJECTIVES:

1.

2.

3.

4.

5.

THREE OBSTACLES: COPING STRATEGY

1.

2.

3.

THREE GAINS:

1.

2.

3.

POSITIVE AFFIRMATION:

One of the biggest risks is to not take a risk, because by not deciding you are still deciding—you're just deciding that you're not going to be the one to take the action that will shape the direction of your life. Our decisions are what define us, and it's exactly that act of self-definition that makes decisions feel so risky. We are a composite of all the decisions we have made in our lives: whom we spend time with, how we spend our days, what we value, what we wear, and how we express ourselves. In fact, much of who we are in this moment is a sum of all our decisions.

During times of transition you may need to make more decisions than usual when you feel least able to or when you feel most tapped out. To minimize the stress of making decisions during a transition, think about your decision-making style when your life is running relatively smoothly. How do you make decisions when things are calm? Do you write a pro and con list and try to weigh things? Do you talk to many people, solicit their ideas, and mull them over? Do you say, "Well, I screw up my decisions anyway, so I'll just wait it out and see what happens?" Do you put yourself in the various situations or aspects of your decision to see which feels right? Or do you stew and wake up at 3:00 a.m. and finally get so frustrated that you just jump into a decision without really thinking about it?

Whom do you know who makes good decisions? Ask them how it is that they make their good decisions. One thing that helps me make my decisions is to look at my values and my life philosophy and ask how each potential choice both meshes and fails to mesh with them.

The best way to make decisions is to look at what you really want from the decision. Let's say I'm faced with a choice of continuing in a job that doesn't fully use my talents or abilities or moving to an unfamiliar city where I'll have a job that more fully meshes with my talents and interests. The choice is between (1) staying in the current job in a city with a pleasant climate where I have lots of friends and connections and know where everything is, but where I'm not satisfied with my job, or (2) moving to an unfamiliar city without an emotional support system, in a climate that I'm not certain I'll like, with a job that sounds much more appealing.

In making this decision I would think, "Okay, what's the best-case scenario and the worst-case scenario for each of those options?" Then I would explore each scenario. In other words, I would ask myself what the worst possible outcome would be for each of the potential decisions. Then I would ask myself, could I live with that? If there was one worst-case scenario that I could live with and one that I couldn't, I would make a mental note of that.

I would also gather as much information as I could about the unknowns in my decision. In this case, I might write to the Chamber of Commerce and ask them about the weather there as well as what services are available to newcomers in the area. I would ask my friends if they know anyone there or how likely it would be for them to come and visit me there. I would also visit the new city to see what it feels like and visit the job site to see if I like it.

Then comes the very personal part of the decision-making process. I would ask myself, "Do these things match my values and my life philosophy?" If my life philosophy says that it is very important for me to be productive and do a lot of good for people, I'd make that an important criterion in making my decision. And if that's not happening in my current job but I would have the chance in the new job, I might be tempted to take the new job because it matches an important piece of my life philosophy.

If one of my first priorities, though, is having connections with friends, then taking the new job might not be as important as staying to maintain those connections. You get to rank the attractiveness of each potential decision based on how it lines up with your values.

So why don't you give it a try now? Your first small step can be to choose something you are struggling to make a decision about. Pull out your values and your life philosophy and look at how they mesh with your potential options. And without having to make a decision for real right now, just play with it and see if your values and life philosophy top the scale in one direction or another.

TIME MANAGEMENT

One of the most important things about moving successfully through transitions is being able to effectively manage your time. In the face of transitions, not only is there much more to contend with and make decisions about, but it also seems that there is less time, partly because when you are stressed, time seems to pass much more quickly than usual, and you don't tend to work as effectively or efficiently. Time management is important in helping you start to accomplish the important objectives and steps toward achieving your goals. Without time management, it is difficult to find time for pursuing the objectives that lead to your goal.

You may find the idea of time management boring and may not want to read this section or deal with this issue for a number of reasons. You may worry that if you manage your time better, you will be required to do more and have more obligations and commitments to meet. Or you may sidestep time management because you believe that if you do it you might actually succeed, and then people will expect it of you all of the time. You may feel that if you successfully use time management you will lose your best excuse for saying no—that you don't have the time. But that isn't the case.

Time management simply helps your life run more smoothly. It does not obligate you to behave in a certain way or to always be there for others. Just because time management creates more time for you doesn't mean you have to spend that time doing things that you don't want to do.

So how do you manage time? One good way is to make a "to do" list. On a separate sheet, list everything you feel you need to accomplish in the next week. After you've completed that, break it down into different categories: Category A is for things you absolutely have to do, Category B is for things that would be helpful to get done that week, and Category C is for things you'd like to get done that week but that aren't essential. Try to divide the tasks evenly between the three categories. Then prioritize the items in each category, listing them in the order of their importance.

Then break down each task into steps. Suppose I need to get a two-page letter to an attorney by the end of the week. What I would do is decide how much I need to write each day of the week in order to meet my deadline. I would need to write an outline and an introductory paragraph, so I'd list these tasks for Monday. Tuesday, I'd write the five main paragraphs. Wednesday, I'd write the summary paragraph. Thursday, I'd type, proofread, and print the letter, and on Friday I'd drop it by the attorney's office. So I would have a sheet of paper that listed Monday through Friday with the project broken down into little pieces to be accomplished each day. I'd do that for each thing I had listed in Category A. The result would list components of all the tasks listed in Category A, with various components assigned to each day of the week. Monday of each week might have the first small bits of several projects. The idea here is that if you break things down into chewable bites, you're less likely to feel overwhelmed and swamped at a time you're already prone to feeling that way.

Make a solemn pact with yourself that as soon as you have completed the crucial items for that day, you will not do any more of the Category A items because those are usually the most stressful things for people. Reward yourself for doing what you needed to do for that day by giving yourself time off for good behavior. You may still want to do something from Category B or C, like getting the car washed or writing a letter to a friend. The important thing is to not penalize yourself for productivity by demanding more and more out of yourself, so that you start to associate being productive with being exhausted.

If you break things down into chewable bites, you're less likely to feel overwhelmed and swamped at a time you're already prone to feeling that way.

You can also use this time management technique for big, long-term projects. If you have something you need to accomplish in 10 months, you can begin with the final due date and then work backward to the present, listing what you need to do each week to eventually meet your final deadline. Each time you accomplish whatever is listed for that week, even if you're done by Tuesday and would have five more days to work on the next piece, stop and give yourself a breather until the next week. By doing this, you are actually rewarding yourself for not procrastinating—sort of like eating the food you like the least first so you can enjoy the rest of your meal.

PULLING YOUR RESOURCES TOGETHER

Let's take a look at everything you've learned about yourself so far through this book.

Q *Chapter One:* Let's look at your own personal transition model. What are the big rocks you face as you go through transitions? List those things here.

A _____

_____

_____

What are your handholds and footholds?

_____

_____

_____

What handholds and footholds would you like to add?

_____

_____

_____

Q

A

Chapter Two: Take another look at your personal patterns in the face of change—how do you handle change? Are there any parts of how you handle change that you'd like to modify to make change go better? Brainstorm some of those ideas now. What small piece could you work on now?

_____

_____

_____

Q

A

Chapter Three: Take a look at your style of dealing with fear and loss. Remember that fear never goes away, and courage is continuing to move forward despite the fear. Knowing that, what are the things you've learned that you can tell yourself when you feel fearful and full of grief? What can you tell yourself that will help you cope better with fear?

_____

_____

_____

Q

Chapter Four: Which emotions tend to get in your way?

_____

_____

A

Which self-defeating behaviors do you need to keep an eye on?

_____

_____

What kinds of coping strategies or alternative behaviors could you substitute for self-defeating behaviors?

_____

_____

_____

What have you learned about communicating your feelings?

_____

_____

How can you best do that when you're under stress?

_____

_____

_____

What can you tell yourself about why it's important to be assertive?

_____

_____

_____

Q
A

Chapter Five: Look at your own self-perception. How do you feel about yourself—what are the good things about yourself?

_____

_____

What things would you like to be more self-accepting about?

_____

_____

_____

In which areas of your life do you engage in approval-seeking behavior?

_____

_____

_____

What could you do to start being more self-approving?

_____

_____

_____

What do you notice about your ease or discomfort in setting boundaries? Where in your life are your boundaries strong? Where would you like them to be sturdier, and how could you strive to create that?

Chapter Six: What relationships in your life have healthy components and what are those components?

What relationships in your life have unhealthy components? How would you like to change them?

Where do you see yourself on the pursuer/distancer spectrum? Do you do more pursuing or more distancing?

What can you do to help yourself negotiate differences in your relationships?

What part of your shadow self would you like to bring into the light and learn to love and accept?

How could accepting those parts of yourself help you live a fuller life?

_____

_____

_____

Q

Chapter Seven: List the core values that you identified in this chapter.

_____

_____

_____

A

How content are you with those values—are there any you'd like to change, delete, or add to?

_____

_____

_____

What do you know about having a positive attitude toward change? What positive things can you tell yourself about change and how can that help you?

_____

_____

_____

What aspects of your life philosophy are you going to hold dearest and use to help you hang on and get through tough times?

_____

_____

_____

How will your life philosophy continue to help you make sense out of your life?

_____

_____

_____

_____

Q

Chapter Eight: What goals would you like to set for yourself in the next five years?

A

What small steps would be important in achieving those goals?

How can you take more responsible risks?

Whom do you know who makes good decisions?

What could you learn from them?

In pulling your resources together, it is important, first, to *look at what you've got going for you* and, second, to *identify potential stumbling blocks.* Just as in the transitions model, examine the big rocks that you must scramble over and explore the handholds and footholds that you can use to brace yourself and move across those rocks. Consider your personal resources, such as beliefs, feelings, or personal qualities (tenacity, flexibility, humor), anything that will help you stay focused and motivated through your transition. Also, consider resources you don't yet possess but would like to acquire. For example, at one time I lacked a group of close-knit friends because most of my friends had moved away. I decided to go out and create a support network for myself—new friends who lived in my city who could be supportive, nurturing, and reciprocal.

It seems that no matter how many resources you may possess, you nonetheless can forget what they are when you're in the midst of a transition. One good way to help yourself remember all of the strengths you have access to is to create your own personal resource list. Your personal resource list will embody nuggets of truth about who you are and will remind you of all that you know and the strengths you can rely on in the face of a new transition.

Q

A

Your list of personal resources

1. Good ways I use my strengths to deal with change:

New ideas I'd like to try:

---

2. Ways I can help myself feel less afraid of change:

New ideas I'd like to try:

---

3. Coping strategies that work well for me:

New ideas I'd like to try:

---

4. Ways I communicate and assert myself:

New ideas I'd like to try:

5. What I like and cherish about myself:

Things I want to learn to like and cherish about myself:

6. Healthy ways that I take good care of myself:

New ideas I'd like to try:

7. What I do well in my relationships:

New ideas I'd like to try:

8. Values that fit me well:

_____

_____

_____

Other values I'd like to explore:

_____

_____

_____

9. What I do to make good decisions:

_____

_____

_____

New ideas I'd like to try:

_____

_____

_____

10. How I manage my time well:

_____

_____

_____

New ideas I'd like to try:

_____

_____

_____

11. Ways I help unstick myself:

_____

_____

_____

New ideas I'd like to try:

_____

_____

_____

12. How I celebrate my efforts and achievements:

....

....

....

New ideas I'd like to try:

....

....

....

STAYING HEALTHY

Another crucial piece in seeing yourself through the transition process is doing your best to stay healthy. Because of their inherently stressful nature and the fact that many times they are changes that have seemingly happened to us rather than ones that we've freely chosen, life transitions can play havoc with our immune systems. This in turn affects our sense of mental, emotional, and physical health and well-being.

Staying healthy means doing what you need to do to protect and nurture yourself in all aspects. It can consist of taking care of your mind by having other people help you with sorting the details of your transition. You can use trusted friends as sounding boards to strategize next steps so you don't feel absolutely alone in your transition process.

Staying healthy includes staying emotionally healthy by having people in your life to whom you can vent your feelings, who encourage you to express how you feel and support you in your growth and change process. It can also include seeking counseling if that's what you need. Staying healthy physically means taking good care of your body; trying to make certain you get enough sleep, healthy food, and vitamins; seeing a doctor when necessary; and exercising even when you don't feel you have the time. Staying healthy spiritually means staying or getting in touch with some guiding sense of what your process means in the big picture. It means knowing why it's important that you are on the planet, what the creative and ordering force in the universe is, and what you are here to contribute.

Staying healthy takes practice and experimenting to discover what works for you. It also requires a commitment to take good care of yourself even when it's not convenient or when others don't approve. It's a matter of listening to, honoring, and being loyal to your needs and feelings.

UNSTICKING YOURSELF WHEN YOU FEEL STUCK

Expect to feel stuck sometimes—like getting wedged between two rocks and being unable to move a hand or a foot. In those moments, you'll probably feel waves of hopelessness, helplessness, frustration, rage, or depression. Whatever emotions you tend to experience when life feels unmanageable, you'll likely feel with the greatest intensity when you feel stuck.

Remember, stuck is not the same as trapped. Stuck means that you're in the process of working yourself out of whatever you've gotten yourself wedged into. Stuck does not mean trapped and contained. You're stuck out on the face of the rock outcrop, not trapped under a pile of boulders, even though it may feel like that.

> *Whatever emotions you tend to experience when life feels unmanageable, you'll likely feel with the greatest intensity when you feel stuck.*

One of the best things you can do when you feel stuck is to ask people you trust, "Help, I'm stuck, can you help unstick me?" Don't keep yourself stuck by thinking you always have to unstick yourself all by yourself. Instead, think of a car stuck on the muddy shoulder of a road. Usually someone else has to attach a tow line to the vehicle to help with the unsticking process. You can't expect to be able to extricate yourself all by yourself every time you're stuck. Sometimes you may be able to by drawing on your coping strategies. But more often you will need the assistance of other people to help free you so you can continue moving through your transition.

It's really important that when you get stuck you stay calm and centered, that you just notice what's going on, and that you try to think of what would help you feel less stuck. Sometimes, what you need to do is just temporarily give yourself a break from whatever you're grappling with and take a time-out. You may have been working so hard at managing your transition that you have lost your clarity and objectivity; or you may be so worn out grappling with a certain issue that you just need a little time off from dealing with it.

Figure 8.2

It's okay to ask for help unsticking yourself.

How much time you can take away from whatever you're stuck on will depend on the specifics of your transition. It might be only a half hour, or it might be a week. Use your own judgment. Ask for help. Pick other people's brains for what they do when they're stuck. What helps me is being physical—exercising or trying to do something different. Just remember, it's all right to be stuck—it doesn't mean you're frozen or trapped. It just means you're stuck for the moment.

Here are some exercises that will help you begin to personalize the information presented in this chapter. Begin by writing yourself a prescription for self-awareness.

R· FOR SELF-AWARENESS

1. Goals I have successfully completed in the past are

   _____

   _____

2. Goals I currently have are

   _____

   _____

3. Areas I feel comfortable in making decisions include

_____

_____

4. Areas in which I struggle with decision making are

_____

_____

5. My response to taking risks usually is

_____

_____

6. Wise ways I use my time are

_____

_____

7. Ways I don't use my time well are

_____

_____

8. Things I do to help myself stay healthy are

_____

_____

9. Things I do that interfere with staying healthy are

_____

_____

10. Ways I help myself when I feel stuck are

_____

_____

11. Ways I stay motivated to reach my goals are

_____

_____

FOR YOUR JOURNAL . . .

1. What did you learn about yourself from this chapter?
2. How does that change things for you or help you make sense of your life?
3. What else do you want to know about yourself?

RECOMMENDED READINGS

Brown, Les. 1995. *The Courage to Live Your Dreams: The Courage to Confront Your Fears.* New York: Harper.

   Teaches how to overcome fears and demonstrates how dealing with fear makes you stronger and increases self-confidence.

Cairo, Jim. 1998. *Motivation and Goal Setting: How to Set and Achieve Goals and Inspire Others.* Franklin Lakes, NJ: Career Press.

   Describes how to define values, create action plans, and maintain motivation even in the face of setbacks.

Simon, Sidney. 1989. *Getting Unstuck.* New York: Time Warner.

   Pinpoints ways to overcome self-imposed barriers to change and ways to take action to create a fulfilling life.

Smith, Hyram. 1995. *The 10 Natural Laws of Successful Time and Life Management.* New York: Warner Books.

   Demonstrates methods for taking control of your schedule and your life through planning, prioritizing, and value analysis, leading to greater satisfaction in life.

Viscott, David. 1977. *Risking.* New York: Simon and Schuster.

   Assists in evaluating risks and provides a handy dos and don'ts checklist for taking reasonable risks.

PREPARING FOR YOUR
NEXT TRANSITION

PREDICTING AND PREPARING
FOR FUTURE TRANSITIONS

Now you've discovered your own personal transition model. The next step is predicting what transitions lie ahead of you. You might want to go back and pull out your lifeline from Chapter One. Think about what future transitions you might be facing and future aspects of your life you would like to have unfold.

What transitions might occur in the process of moving forward with your life? Just make a list without worrying about whether or not it is accurate. Which of those transitions pertain only to you and which transitions involve and affect other people? Which transitions do you see as positive and which do you see as less positive or negative?

Preparing for a future transition is much like preparing to take a long trip. There are several ways to leave on a trip. You can leave spontaneously at the last minute, jumping into whatever kind of transportation you're departing in, and just hope you have what you need, dealing with anything you have overlooked along the way. Or you can prepare for the trip in advance, making lists of things you want to include and making certain you have everything packed and that you're leaving well-prepared with everything you can anticipate needing.

Similarly, you can prepare for future transitions by making a list of what to take on your transition journey—your personal resource list you created in Chapter Eight. Know where your trouble sports are and arrange to minimize those trouble spots by using your resources. It's important to have a clear sense of having packed your personal resources to take along with you for your transition process. For example, if you know the kids are leaving home for college and that's going to be hard on you, even though it's not going to happen for another five years, you can plan preventive action to prepare for this transition. Perhaps you want to start to expand your own life and circle of friends and activities. Or perhaps you can weave in or create some special family traditions while the kids are still at home.

Predicting and preparing for transitions also means doing things so you don't feel surprised or traumatized by transitions that you knew would inevitably occur. Retirement is a transition that many people find difficult. Because it's frightening to think about the aging process or no longer working, many people try to dodge their awareness of retirement. If you do that, you can wake up one morning at age 65 and realize that you haven't prepared for the future. You an feel overwhelmed when faced with how you're going to occupy your time and how you're going to financially care for yourself in the future.

Preparing for a future transition is much like preparing to take a long trip.

Alternately, you can start planning ahead of time by saying, "What situation do I want to be in by the time I'm 65?" Once you've asked yourself this question, you can then determine what your goals are for your future transition, and then you can use the action plan format discussed in Chapter Eight to help you take concrete action towards being prepared for upcoming transitions. Doing this allows your life to flow more smoothly from change to change as you are steadily, slowly, and consistently working on aspects of your transitions.

Obviously, you have no way of predicting or being prepared for some transitions. In those cases it would be helpful to pull out your personal resource list from Chapter Eight and remember all the things you learned from this book and your own process. You may need to relabel the specific rocks and handholds to accurately represent each new transition. Also remember that you have many personal resources you can rely on and new ones you can develop, and that you know how to move through this process.

TROUBLESHOOTING POTENTIAL OBSTACLES IN ADVANCE

One of the things that can make transitions tough is that often you're face to face with a looming boulder before you've had a chance to stand back and think about what part of it would be the most effective to tackle first. That's why trying to troubleshoot obstacles in advance is helpful.

What you can do at the first hint that a transition is coming up is to ask yourself, "What things could make this upcoming transition especially difficult?" Don't worry about whether they are realistic or if they have only a one percent likelihood of happening; just list anything that you're concerned about.

Troubleshooting potential obstacles in advance allows you to face actual obstacles from a place of calm rather than from an out-of-control place of crisis.

On the other half of the sheet of paper, list anything you think might even slightly help minimize the obstacles. Your list can include anything that would work for you, such as telling yourself to feel and think something differently in regard to dealing with that obstacle. Just see what you can generate.

When you reach moments where you feel stuck, grab a friend or other caring people around you and ask what they think and how they would tackle that obstacle. If some people say, "That's a stupid thing to be worried about," explain to them that this isn't about being realistic, this is about trying to have as many tools in your kit as possible so that you have already mentally rehearsed dealing with the obstacles.

This way, when an obstacle shows up, whether it's one on your list or a different one, you're already mentally and emotionally practiced in saying, "Hmm, there's an obstacle, what might work?" And you also have created a healthy pattern of being able to generate ways of dealing with obstacles and soliciting input and advice from other people. You don't necessarily take others' advice; you just ask for it and consider it as one way of expanding your options.

Troubleshooting potential obstacles in advance allows you to face actual obstacles from a place of calm rather than from an out-of-control place of crisis. If you expect obstacles and prepare for them by having your own plan for dealing with them, they'll feel less traumatizing, even if you're not thrilled at their appearance in your life.

SEEKING OUTSIDE HELP

How do you know if a transition or its emotional effects are outside the realm of something that you can deal with by yourself, with the help of this book, or with the help of a loved one? The gauge I tell people to

Figure 9.1

Becky faces her next obstacle calmly, thanks to troubleshooting it earlier.

use when they ask me, "Do you think I need to see a counselor?" is to help them look at whether their day-to-day life is severely disrupted.

You may feel a lot of strong, intense emotions and at the same time be able to function quite well, get up in the morning and go where you need to go, do your daily tasks, sleep relatively well, eat reasonably well, and still satisfy all of your obligations. You may feel miserable while you're doing it but still be able to function day to day. For an individual in that situation, I would say it's really up to the person—seeing a counselor might help alleviate those miserable feelings much sooner and help you move through them faster to reach resolution. If your life is running reasonably or functionally well, I'd say it's up to you.

For someone whose life is disrupted, whether moderately or severely, outside help can really assist in creating some structure. Outside help can create a container for all of the fears and intense emotions that come up during transitions. It can help you develop a framework that says, "Okay, this is step one, this is step two," making sense out of all of the hurt and painful feelings, and providing you with a companion through the process.

In certain aspects of the transition process, especially the fear and grief, many of us need a companion to keep us company and to let us know that we're not alone. Even though we're the ones who have to do the work, feel the feelings, and do the growing, it helps to have someone as a witness, someone who expresses the fact that they understand our pain, who wants us to feel better, and who believes in our ability to persevere.

If your life is being substantially disrupted, I encourage you to look into whatever counseling options are available in your community. Most communities offer low-cost or free counseling at community mental health agencies to assist you in times of transition.

CELEBRATING EFFORT AND ACHIEVEMENT

Part of the joy of diving off the transition cliff, hitting the warm, balmy water, and paddling for the other side is celebrating your effort that got you to the top, to the place where you could launch into the next phase of your life. In going through transitions, it's easy to get caught up with surviving moment to moment and focusing on just making it to the end of the transition. Remember that it's crucial to acknowledge and approve of yourself for how hard you worked, how scared you were, and for the fact that you stayed in there and kept going. Give yourself credit for how resilient you are, for how powerful you are to face up to all of the things you didn't want to look at but did, and how you thereby made your transition go more smoothly. Value and honor the willpower, effort, endurance, strength, and hope that you drew upon to move through this transition.

* *

One of the nicest things you can do to celebrate your efforts and achievements is to create a celebration calendar.

* *

Acknowledge yourself for all the actions and steps you took, even when you didn't believe in them in the moment. Applaud yourself for choosing to put one foot in front of the other, for having one breath follow another, and for the fact that you stayed in there, you kept showing up, you kept suiting up, and you kept saying, "I'm still in the game—I haven't given up."

Remember to celebrate the fact that you possess the will, the power, the energy, and the life force to keep moving through changing, hard, painful, difficult times. Feel proud that you are enduring and that you have wisdom and worth. Celebrate all that you have achieved: the new things you learned about yourself, the old behaviors that no longer work for you that you've let go of, the new resources that you've added to your life, the old pain that you dealt with and let go of, the grieving you did that you thought would never end, and the new self that emerged. Compliment yourself for accomplishing another major step in your life and for finding new power, new self-awareness, and new strengths that you didn't know existed.

One of the nicest things you can do to celebrate your efforts and achievements is to create a celebration calendar. Every time you achieve something or put out a special effort, make a small note of it on a calendar or date book. And each year, add the previous year's celebrations to the current calendar. Keep adding notations; within a few years each day will be a celebration day—a reminder of you and your strengths, your abilities, your vision, and your belief in yourself. It's also a reminder of your knowledge that no matter what happens, you are going to continue forward, to grow, learn, love yourself and others well, and move on into a full, enriching, wonderful, changeable life.

Congratulations! You have successfully journeyed through information and exercises designed to assist you in moving more smoothly

Figure 9.2

You made it—congratulations!

through your life transitions. I've included one final statement of self-awareness, with the intent that you end your interaction with this book by powerfully celebrating yourself.

STATEMENT OF SELF-AWARENESS

1. I acknowledge and approve of myself for the following efforts:

   _____

   _____

   _____

   _____

   _____

   _____

2. I acknowledge and approve of myself for these achievements:

   _____

   _____

   _____

   _____

   _____

   _____

3. I celebrate my growth in the following areas:

_____

_____

_____

_____

4. I celebrate myself for all of the wonderful things I am, with a few of those wonderful things being:

_____

_____

_____

_____

NOTES/JOURNAL

NOTES/JOURNAL

NOTES/JOURNAL

NOTES/JOURNAL

NOTES/JOURNAL

NOTES/JOURNAL

NOTES/JOURNAL

NOTES/JOURNAL

INDEX